SUPPER WITH THE SHEPHERD KING

Thoughts on Psalm 23

BY
LT. COLONEL DAN JENNINGS

FOREWORD BY
LT. COLONEL LESA DAVIS

CREST BOOKS

Copyright © 2023 by The Salvation Army

Published by Crest Books

Crest Books
The Salvation Army National Headquarters
615 Slaters Lane
Alexandria, VA 22314
Phone: 703-684-5523

Lt. Colonel Lesa Davis, *Editor-in-Chief*
Maryam Outlaw, *Editorial Assistant*
Staci Williams, *Graphic Designer*

ISBN print: 978-1-946709-14-1

Unless otherwise indicated, all Scripture quotations are taken from the Holy Bible, New Living Translation, Copyright © 1996, 2004, 2015 by Tyndale House Foundation. Used by permission of Tyndale House Publishers, Inc., Carol Stream, Illinois 60188. All rights reserved.

All rights reserved. No part of this publication may be reproduced, stored in a retrieval system, or transmitted in any form or by any means without prior written permission of the publisher. Exceptions are brief quotations in printed reviews.

Contents

Foreword v
Acknowledgements vii
Introduction 1

Chapter 1: The Lord is My Shepherd 7

Chapter 2: Shepherd-King 15

Chapter 3: The Roles of the Shepherd 25

Chapter 4: I Shall Not Want 59

Chapter 5: Four Blessings 67

Chapter 6: Very Deep Shadows 87

Chapter 7: You Are With Me 97

Chapter 8: Rod and Staff 105

Chapter 9: You Prepare a Table Before Me 113

Chapter 10: You Anoint My Head With Oil 121

Chapter 11: Goodness and Mercy 137

Chapter 12: I Shall Dwell in the House of the Lord Forever 145

Final Thoughts 151

Foreword

"Do you want to grab a bite to eat?"

That's an invitation that my husband and I have both extended and accepted countless times, many of them involving Lt. Colonel Dan Jennings and his wife Dorene. With the Jennings, we have enjoyed everything from early morning hotel breakfast buffets to late-night treats at a Midwest frozen custard stand. The places and the food have run the gamut from fine dining to questionable greasy spoons, but the time around the table with Dan and Dorene has never disappointed.

In this book, Lt. Colonel Jennings invites readers to a banquet table prepared by the Lord Himself and shared by His people through time and history. Through a thoughtful look at Psalm 23, readers will come to see this well-loved psalm with fresh eyes. This book will move it from that psalm you always hear at funerals to an exploration of a deeply personal relationship with the Shepherd King who pursues, protects, and provides for His sheep.

One of the challenges of Psalm 23 is its familiarity. Many readers will have memorized it somewhere along the way. Even those who rarely read the Bible or attend a church service could probably recite at least the first couple of lines. That familiarity can cause even the most faithful of us to miss much of the richness of this beautiful Scripture. Using stories and metaphors, along with Hebrew word studies and reflective questions, Jennings corrects that by drawing us into the world of an Old Testament shepherd and at the same time, invites us to see ourselves and our very modern lives through the lens of this ancient psalm. Whether you find yourself resting in green pastures or fighting your way through the valley of shadows, this book will help you discern the presence of the God who relentlessly pursues and welcomes all who will follow Him.

I am especially appreciative of the built-in pauses for reflection and the practical life applications drawn by the author. I believe you, the reader, will come away from this book refreshed, renewed, and more able to follow the Great Shepherd than ever before.

So, do you want to grab a bite to eat? If you're ready for an unforgettable feast, this book will usher you to the table of the Shepherd King.

Lt. Colonel Lesa Davis
Director of Publications
National Headquarters

Acknowledgments

This project has been on my heart for some time. There have been fits and starts along the way. At times I doubted that it would ever come together. I want to thank Commissioner Merle Heatwole, who challenged me to be a good steward of my seminary education and give thought to writing a book. I am grateful to the team at *The War Cry*, who published a series of articles I wrote on the twenty-third psalm in the Bible Study section of the magazine. These articles have become the seeds that sprouted into this book. I also wish to acknowledge my wife, Dorene, who has encouraged me along the way and supported my writing efforts. I need to thank those who graciously agreed to read the early versions of this book and offered guidance and direction that has proved invaluable. I want to give particular thanks to Judy Yttrevold, Lt. Colonel Lesa Davis, and Lt. Colonel Dean Pallant for their gracious editorial contributions.

Thank you for starting to read this book. I invite you on a journey through Psalm 23. I pray the Holy Spirit will speak to you directly. I have included many opportunities to pause and reflect throughout the book. Sometimes there are questions posed, but at other times, there is simply the opportunity to pause, reflect, and listen to the still, small voice of the Great Shepherd who calls all of us, every day, if we have ears to listen.

Finally, I thank the Lord for His gift of scripture that is alive and speaks to our hearts today in new and fresh ways. Psalm 23 is an excellent example of ancient words that speak to a contemporary audience with imagery and truth that impacts our world.

Introduction

"The LORD is my shepherd;
I have all that I need.
He lets me rest in green meadows;
He leads me beside peaceful streams.
He renews my strength.
He guides me along right paths,
bringing honor to his name.
Even when I walk
through the darkest valley,
I will not be afraid,
for you are close beside me.
Your rod and your staff
protect and comfort me.
You prepare a feast for me
in the presence of my enemies.
You honor me by anointing my head with oil.
My cup overflows with blessings.
Surely your goodness and unfailing love will pursue me
all the days of my life,
and I will live in the house of the LORD
forever."

-Psalm 23:1-6

Psalm 23 is, perhaps, the most recognizable chapter throughout all Christian Scripture. One could argue effectively that John 3:16 is the most recognized verse. However, Psalm 23 is potentially the most recognizable chapter. If you are like me, you cannot count the number of times that you have heard this passage read at a Christian funeral or graveside service. I myself have even contributed to the number of times this passage has been used in these types of gatherings. For a pastor who is seeking to minister to families who have gathered to celebrate the life of a loved one, Psalm 23 is a go-to passage. The words of this psalm have brought comfort and peace to grieving families during times of difficult loss. They are rich and powerful, full of imagery and meaning.

It is my hope that this book serves to rescue this psalm from its relegation to the graveside and provide a broader perspective of what is revealed about God within its verses. Interestingly, the ceremony book of The Salvation Army suggests that Psalm 23 is an appropriate reading for weddings as well as funerals. I am not sure if I have ever heard this psalm quoted at a wedding. Who wants to think about walking through the shadow of death while walking down the aisle? The point that the ceremony book makes is valid, however. The psalm is a rich and full description of who God is in relationship to believers and is appropriate outside of funeral services. Without diminishing its ministry to the bereaved, let's extricate it from its reputation as only "the funeral psalm." Throughout this book we will explore the psalm and ask God's Holy Spirit to reveal its words to us in a new and fresh way. Try for a moment to forget that you know the words by heart and hear them again as if for the first time. Allow the metaphorical words of Psalm 23 to conjure up in your mind a fresh image of God as a Shepherd, King, and Host of the banquet. Try to approach Psalm 23 with fresh eyes and let it say something new to you.

The words of this psalm are skillfully crafted and arranged to help the reader capture a vivid picture of the invisible God. When one reads the carefully curated words of Psalm 23, one can imagine the gloomy and frightening path that leads through the valley of the shadow of death. It makes you cringe to think about death's rotten, icy fingers stretching out to take hold of you. With any imagination, we can hear the haunting hoot of an owl during the night watch. We can imagine the putrid aroma that would waft through a place associated with death, imagine the temperature change as we descend together with the writer into the deep valley starved of sunlight, enveloped in ever darkening shadows. In contrast, we can also imagine the opulence and wonder of the banquet table prepared by the Lord. Imagine a table finely adorned and overflowing with lavish foods and erupting with the wonderful smells of roasted meats and freshly baked breads. The picture painted by the psalmist goes beyond dismal valleys and luscious feasts. The word-picture painted in this psalm is one of God Himself. The picture is born out of God's desire for self-disclosure. This is to say that Psalm 23 is a wonderful example of God's personal revelation of His nature to mankind. As you read through the psalm, allow God's Holy Spirit to peel back the layers that obscure our vision and help you discover what it reveals about God's incredibly gracious, loving, and restorative nature. Because of the limitation of human understanding and perspective, God chooses the metaphor, or at least inspires the writer of the psalm in such a way that the metaphor becomes the medium. The writer of Psalm 23 employs two primary metaphorical images in this chapter to reveal God's nature. The images are remarkably different from each other. They are images that the first readers of the psalm would have understood well. The images are based in humanity, which helps the reader to relate to them, and portray God's nature through the lens of human endeavors. The first metaphor is that of a shepherd and the second is host of a banquet. This unlikely pair of metaphors are held together by their purpose of illuminating the main character of Scripture, the Lord. Not only to shed light on the Lord, but also to reveal key insights regarding His intention towards humanity. The Lord desires to lead and to bless mankind. He lets us know that He is the Shepherd and that we are the sheep under His care.

Both metaphors invite the reader to see God's divine restorative character. As one commentator has noted, "Using the images of a shepherd and a gracious host, David reflected on the many benefits the Lord gave him in the dangers of life, and concluded that God's persistent, loving protection would restore him to full communion."[1] David was aware of the need for a deity able to bring about the restoration of the nation of Israel. David was also painfully aware of his own shortcomings and, as such, embraced his own need of restoration. Even in the darkest times of Israel's history and in David's lowest moments, the Lord stands as the ever-present, gracious Shepherd and Provider—a host who opens His home and heart to him. David recognized these important hallmarks of the character of the Lord and helps us, the readers of this psalm, to know the immeasurable joy of being invited to the Lord's banquet table as welcome and honored guests.

The opening chapter of this book will look closely at the first of the metaphors used in this psalm and explore how the Shepherd relates to God's desire to project a self-disclosing image towards mankind. Both the Shepherd and the Lord of the banquet are powerfully rich imagery worth our consideration. Now let's set aside our familiarity with these words and hear them fresh.

CHAPTER 1
THE LORD IS MY SHEPHERD

*"I am the good shepherd. I know my own and
my own know me…" —John 10:14*

I grew up in the state of Kansas, and although I lived in the city, the country was never far away. I can still remember the weekend trips with my parents to my uncle's farm. The ride was less than thirty minutes, but it transported us to a remarkably different world. The farm had a few cows, an old mini horse, a goose, a few goats, and a busy flock of chickens. By any measure of farming, this was a small outfit. However, it seemed that my uncle and aunt were always busy with one situation or another that had to do with the animals they were responsible for. My conclusion as a young person was that taking care of animals is a very busy venture. If you ask any shepherd, they will whole-heartedly agree. Despite the difficulties and massive efforts of farming, ranching, and shepherding, it is a profession that many still embrace. There remains a magnetic draw for some to work the earth. There is something that speaks to the souls of those who choose this life. There are amazing blessings received when outside in God's nature. There is something rewarding about the care of animals. Some people are simply built for this kind of life. This was, without a doubt, the case for my aunt and uncle. It has been many years since I visited that farm, but the sights and smells still flood back to me as I remember those youthful adventures. As a boy, I could not have fully appreciated the chore it was for my aunt and uncle to keep up with the farm and the animals. While most of us are familiar with the iconic image of a shepherd, we probably do not fully appreciate all that goes into the craft of shepherding.

A few years ago, I had the great experience of going on a Holy Land tour to explore Israel and see the important biblical sites. During the tour, our bus snaked its way down the narrow roads of a small rural village in Israel as the passengers held their breaths, hoping that the bus would somehow become smaller. I remember being impressed with the driver's skill in maneuvering such a large vehicle through the tight turns of the village. At one point, as we were on the outskirts of this village, we noticed a shepherd who was leading her flock along the road. The bus stopped as the shepherd and her flock made their way across, and it was a treat for us on the bus to see the shepherd leading her sheep. Her face was weathered from the elements and the hard work of shepherding. The scene was something of a stark contrast between the occupants on the bus and the shepherd. We were in comfortable seats enjoying an air-conditioned bus ride. She was in the elements. She was practicing an ancient craft long employed in the region. We were reaching for digital cameras and smart phones to capture this moment, then launch the images into cyberspace to land on social media pages halfway around the world. This was an intersection of the ancient and modern. It occurred to me that this shepherd was leading her sheep in such a way that was probably very similar to that of her ancient ancestors, sans the interrupting tour bus and snapping pictures.

The sheep followed the shepherd as she whistled and tapped her crook on the ground. They were seemingly unaffected by our presence and moved like a wind-swept cloud just behind the shepherd. It was a merging of two distinctly different worlds, accomplishing a couple of things. For one, the pilgrims on our bus were able to capture terrific pictures of an authentic shepherd for our travelogues. But secondly, the brief encounter with the Israeli shepherd brought to mind just how prevalent the imagery of the shepherd is throughout Scripture.

The notion of shepherding is as old as the biblical narrative itself. When you give it some thought and careful investigation, you'll be amazed by the number of shepherds that are featured in the Bible. Here are several that come to mind:

- When **Adam** was given dominion over creation, in a sense, he became the shepherd of all the creatures of the earth. Adam was given the task of naming each species of animal.

- Adam's son, **Abel**, was a "keeper of sheep" (Genesis 4).

- **Abraham** is described in Genesis 13 as "rich in livestock."

- **Isaac** had possessions of flocks and herds (Genesis 26).

- **Jacob** was a skilled "breeder of sheep" (Genesis 30).

- **Rachel** was a shepherdess of her father's sheep (Genesis 29).

- **Joseph**, before he was sold into slavery by his brothers, was described as "tending the flocks" (Genesis 37:2 NIV).

- **Moses** spent forty years in the Transjordan wilderness of Midian developing his vocation of shepherding, which was helpful as he began his task of leading the Israelites out of Egypt. (While Moses shepherded the Israelites, God made his own presence known to the wandering immigrants with smoke and fire. It has been described by the nineteenth-century theologian Henry Soltau this way: "The pillar of cloud by day and [fire] by night, seem to have somewhat symbolized this shepherd care of the Lord. It was a guide, a [defense], a shelter, a light, a place of intercourse with God, from whence He spoke, and from whence He manifested His power and His glory."[2])

Given Israel's familiarity with the occupation of shepherding and the importance of the trade to the ancient Near East culture, the shepherd metaphor is an ideal image for the Lord to reveal Himself to Israel. It is not surprising that David employs the image as a literary tool in Psalm 23. In fact, many of the Bible's writers employed the shepherd image liberally when conveying their important messages. Within the ancient oral traditions of passing along sacred concepts, imagery was an important way to capture something of the essence of God.

Biblical images of God include animal references such as a bear (Hosea 13), a mother hen (Matthew 23), a lion (Job 10 & Proverbs 19), a lamb (Isaiah 53, John 1, 1 Peter 1), a dove (Matthew 3), and an ox or bull (Numbers 24).

In addition to those images, there are also references to God taken from the elements of the natural world, including a rock (Psalm 18:2), a fountain (Proverbs 13:14), the sun (Psalms 84:11, John 8), a vine (John 15:5), and a root (Isaiah 11:10).

Still, there are a number of vocational references to the Lord as well: King, Soldier, Sculptor, Vinedresser. Each of these captures a facet of the nature of the Lord. Each is limited in its ability to communicate an accurate description of the Lord. However, each engages our creativity and imagination, and enriches our ability to understand something of who the Lord is and how He relates to us and creation itself.

Of all of the above descriptors of who the Lord is, the Shepherd is one of the most intimate and relevant metaphors used. It was certainly relevant to David and resonated with the early readers of this psalm. As we course our way through Psalm 23, it will be important to give some purposeful attention to this image, as it is used by David to describe the nature of the Lord as it has been revealed to him. Even now, early in your reading of this book, take some time to reflect on this particular metaphor. These images can be a very powerful tool in helping the reader to understand the nature and truth being conveyed about who the Lord is. After all, it can be a difficult thing to explain the mysterious attributes of an eternal God to mortal beings. This image of a shepherd can inform the reader of the nature of the Lord and at the same time, help them to realize the interplay between the immortal God and humans, who are a part of the creation.

This passage speaks to the reader in a theological way—that is, the passage speaks about the Lord. The Lord is a shepherd. No metaphor is entirely perfect, and in some ways this one is not without its flaws. However, it does a good job in helping us to understand a key aspect or facet of who the Lord is. The Lord is our Shepherd.

The passages also speak to the reader in an ecclesiological manner. This is to say that the passages tell us something about ourselves as believers and as the Church. If The Lord is our Shepherd, the implication is that we are His sheep. Later in the psalms, David affirms this notion by stating that we are the "sheep" under His care (Psalm 95).

As we think closely about sheep and their shepherd, it helps us to understand the relation between the human and the divine. It underscores our reliance on a caring God who acts as our Shepherd.

It is the relationship between the divine and human that I think is so well communicated by the use of the shepherd and sheep imagery. The sheep find their purpose, comfort, safety, peace, substance, joy, vocation, affection, and care from the shepherd. The shepherd finds his or her purpose, vocation, fulfilment, and joy in tending the sheep. It is tempting to say that there is a symbiotic relationship between the sheep and the shepherd. However, the role of the shepherd clearly has an elevated sense of responsibility and significance. However, knowing that there is more responsibility on the shoulders of the shepherd does not discount the reality of a significant relationship here. Sheep who have no shepherd are wearied and harassed creatures destined for disaster. Shepherds without sheep lack purpose and fail to live up to the moniker by which they are identified.

It is time to embrace the usage of the metaphor and approach Psalm 23 with an expectation of discovery. Try to hear this Psalm in a way that acknowledges its literary form and allow David to introduce you to the Lord who is his Shepherd. Think about what the metaphor means to David. Consider what that image might mean to you to have a God who is represented by the image of a shepherd. Read over the list of other ways the Bible illustrates the nature of God, from the natural world to the animal kingdom.

Adopting a different posture and pace as you read Psalm 23 may be helpful to you as you seek to get to know this God who is also the Shepherd. Ask yourself lots of questions. Ask the Spirit to open your mind so as to see the Lord in the way David has conceived of Him in this Psalm.

You may have to constrain some of your mind's preexisting notions or images of farming and shepherding in order to see David's perspective of a shepherd. It is a worthwhile exercise and I hope you find it to be both challenging and informative. As you consider the questions to ask yourself, here are some that may help get the process rolling:

Pause for Reflection

- Of all the images listed above, which ones resonate most with you?

- What is the first image that comes to your mind when you hear the word "shepherd"?

- What does it mean to you to know that the Lord is your Shepherd?

- How did Abraham's time tending his father-in-law's flock in the wilderness prepare him for leading the children of Israel out of Egypt?

CHAPTER 2
SHEPHERD-KING

"For thus says the Lord God: Behold, I, I myself will search for my sheep and will seek them out." –Ezekiel 34:11

David's utilization of "the shepherd" in Psalm 23 doesn't feel contrived or out of place. In fact, the subject naturally flows from the life of David. Of course he chose the metaphor of a shepherd to describe the Lord. The idea of shepherding would have been both familiar and comfortable for David. In Psalm 23, he overlays this familiar image of the shepherd with his understanding of YHWH. The resulting image is that of the God who is both Israel's King and Shepherd. The image of the shepherd-king is not uniquely employed in describing the divine. In Hebrew history, it was invoked as a descriptor of Israel's kings. David was one of Israel's most prolific kings. It is important to note that before David was anointed as king over Israel, he was appointed as shepherd over his father's flock. The lessons that David learned caring for his father's sheep on the Bethlehem hillsides would serve him well as he took on the responsibility of shepherding God's people. The biblical shepherd-king motif is captured in the Book of 2 Samuel as David takes on the role. The people of Israel had placed their hope in David to reunite the fractured nation. In 2 Samuel 5, the Israelites gathered at Hebron for David's anointing and reminded him that "…The Lord said to you, 'You shall be shepherd of my people Israel, and you shall be prince over Israel'" (2 Samuel 5:2). This dual role of both shepherd and king was a fitting image for David, as well as those who subsequently would be given the responsibility to govern over Israel. Of all the kings of Israel, notwithstanding Jesus Himself, David embodied the image of the shepherd-king most completely.

The image of the shepherd-king is not, however, exclusive to Israel. Despite how poignant the imagery was for Israel, the metaphor was employed nearly universally at the time. The kings of the Near East were spoken about as shepherd-kings. Matthew Montonini pointed out that in eighteenth-century BC, "Hammurabi, the famed king of Babylon, [was] given this moniker in several places of the prologue and epilogue of his law code."[3] It was not uncommon for the people of Near Eastern culture to refer to their monarchs and deities as shepherds and there has even been academic debate over how much of the Jewish covenant code was influenced or borrowed from Near Eastern sources such as the Laws of Hammurabi. So, it's hard to imagine that David's poetic imagery of YHWH as shepherd and king was not in some way influenced by the culture of the Near East.

The shepherd-king as an image of political and spiritual leadership was also embraced by Israel's neighbors, the Egyptians. "Ancient Egypt went further than any other society on record in the direction of making what we have called the royal metaphor a social force. The Pharaoh was not only the shepherd of his people, high priest as well as king, but also an incarnate god."[4] The artwork of ancient Egypt has captured images of the pharaohs holding shepherd crooks, symbolizing their role as the shepherd of the people. For the nations of the Near East, the roles of shepherd and king were inseparable.

While other kingdoms during the time of Davidic rule saw their monarchs and deities as shepherds and kings, the image of YHWH as the Shepherd-King of the people of Israel is not to be undermined. Rather, it helped to set the context for who YHWH is in relationship to those who reside under His leadership and care. The metaphor allows the contemporary reader of this psalm to easily understand the dual role that YHWH held for the Jewish people. The Lord demonstrated a caring and shepherd-like responsibility for the Israelites and was the revered deity of the nation of Israel. This relationship between the Lord as Shepherd and King and the people of Israel would serve as a pattern for David and others who would be given the mantle of leadership over Israel as its shepherd-king. Not only did it serve as a pattern, but it also served as a standard to which every king or leader would be measured.

It is right and good to think of YHWH as the shepherd of Israel, even if the shepherd image is neither original nor exclusive. David's use of the shepherd image in Psalm 23 provides for us a view of the nature of the God of Israel. One of the key characteristics of the Lord, communicated by the use of shepherd imagery, is that He is a God who cares for His people. It is this notion that has influenced commentary writers to note that David's use of shepherd imagery to describe God illustrates David's affirmation that it is God "who uniformly and graciously provides for and guides"[5] all of creation. Like a shepherd that provides continual and capable care of the flock, God provides and cares for all of creation. Psalm 23 reminds Israel of the divine care that they receive.

David's use of the shepherd as a description of the Lord taps into the shepherd-king motif. It helps the reader to appreciate that the Lord is the caretaker of all creation. The reader of the psalm is encouraged to take comfort in the understanding that

God cares for them as a shepherd cares for their sheep. In other places in the Book of Psalms, we see the psalmist call out to God and invoke His shepherd nature. In Psalm 28:9, God is asked to be Israel's "shepherd and carry them forever." In Psalm 80, God is called the "Shepherd of Israel." This idea of God being the shepherd of His people has carried forward into the world that you and I live in. God's care and provision for creation is not limited to an Old Testament notion of who God is. We are recipients of God's shepherd-like provision, too. The Lord is our Shepherd and our King. We live under God's watchful eye and are beneficiaries of His care and protection.

Pause for reflection

- Why were the kings of the Ancient Near East also considered to be shepherds?

- Do you think that David's view of the Lord as his Shepherd is influenced by his culture? If so, in what ways?

While the shepherd-king image is referenced all throughout the Old Testament of the Bible, it is worth momentarily diverting from Psalm 23 to briefly consider the shepherd theme within the New Testament, too. One of the striking differences, particularly seen in the gospels, is that the New Testament shepherd image is primarily Christological.

NEW TESTAMENT SHEPHERD

The most overt ways in which the New Testament carries forward the Old Testament concept of God as the Shepherd-King is in the person of Jesus Christ. In the gospels we see that Christ has compassion on the crowds of people who were spiritually lost and without a shepherd (Matthew 9:36; Mark 6:34). Jesus describes Himself as the "Good Shepherd" three times in Chapter 10 of the Book of John (vv 1, 11, 14). Jesus becomes the embodiment, within the chapters of the New Testament, of what David describes in Psalm 23. Jesus cares for His people as a shepherd cares for his sheep.

In John 10 we see the extraordinary compassion that Jesus has for humanity as the Good Shepherd. Jesus understands and embraces the sacrificial role of the shepherds and pledges to lay down His own life for those who are His sheep (v 15). Jesus also demonstrates a radical inclusivity in exclaiming that He has "other sheep" (v 16). Jesus describes His relationship with the sheep as one in which He speaks and the sheep both listen and follow. He invites others to join Him in the critical role of shepherding as He instructs Peter to "feed [his] sheep" (v 21). Clearly, the idea of a divine shepherd is not abandoned in the writings of the New Testament. If anything, it is illustrated beautifully in the life of Jesus as He shepherded those who flocked to Him.

As we try to understand David's image of God as the Shepherd-King in light of what we read of Jesus as the Good Shepherd in the New Testament, it is critical to understand that Jesus is not simply adopting the qualities or mimicking a shepherd of the Old Testament. Jesus is the complete and full embodiment of the Shepherd-King David speaks about in Psalm 23. It is not sufficient to say that Jesus is *like* the shepherd of Psalm 23. Jesus *is* the Shepherd-King. An apostolic reading of the Old Testament sees Jesus throughout all of Scripture, and therefore the Shepherd-King in this psalm.

The apostolic approach to reading the Old Testament is congruent with a trinitarian view of the Bible. Viewing Scripture through a trinitarian lens acknowledges the inseparability of each of the persons of the Trinity—Father, Son, and Spirit. It allows the reader to see the Davidic Shepherd not singularly as a character of the Old Testament, but as present in the person of Jesus Christ throughout the entirety of Scripture. Similarly, we can attribute the role of the Shepherd-King to the Spirit as well. One of the primary ways in which we see the Spirit interact with humanity is in divine leadership. The Holy Spirit can be seen clearly as a shepherd. Samuel Logan Brengle, the great holiness theologian of the Army's earliest days, certainly makes the connection. He writes:

> It is the work of the Holy Spirit to guide the people of God through the uncertainties and dangers and duties of this life to their home in Heaven. When He led the children of Israel out of Egypt, by the hand of Moses, He guided them through the waste, mountainous wilderness, in a pillar of cloud by day and of fire by night, thus assuring their comfort and safety. And this was but a type of His perpetual spiritual guidance of His people.[6]

I have given much thought to the shepherds during the past several Advent seasons. No Advent season is complete without attending at least one Christmas pageant. Some of them are elaborate and even include live animals. Some Christmas pageants are a bit less of a spectacle and involve only a few children rehearsing the story for the congregation.

Of all the costumes that are required to pull off even the smallest pageant, a shepherd's is, arguably, the easiest of them to manufacture. All you need is a bathrobe, a stick long enough to serve as a shepherd's staff, and a willing child to play the role.

In churches across the globe, children are dramatically transformed into shepherds. They are instantly recognized by the congregation and play their roles to perfection by milling around the platform while Luke 2 is read.

As a corps officer, I helped some of the children to take advantage of the incredible ability to disguise oneself as a shepherd during one of our Christmas pageants. We draped some of the young people in robes and outfitted them with their shepherds' crooks, and even completed the transformation by providing them with a real-life sheep. We also provided a real-life shepherd to ensure that things did not get out of control. The planning was carefully done and the transformation was complete, but the children learned quickly that shepherding is not an easy vocation and that sheep have their own aromatic ... uniqueness. One of the children could not contain his astonishment with the creature and declared loudly during the pageant, "This sheep stinks!" It was an instant classic and years later, many of us still recount the service with a smile.

In the last decade of Christian preaching, it has become popular to point out the very humble state of shepherds in the first century. Many contrast the incredible news of the Savior's birth with the lowly audience who, owing to their role as a shepherd, would have been seen as unclean by rabbinical standards and ineligible for temple worship. The natural dichotomy between the heights of divinity and one of the lowest forms of humanity is irresistible to some sermon writers.

Shepherding was not the most desirable job to have. During the first century, there were serious societal deficits to the vocation. However, Jesus had no hesitation in identifying Himself with these modest keepers of sheep. Jesus identifies Himself as the Good Shepherd. Psalm 23 admires the role of a shepherd, ascribing it to the Lord. As noted earlier, the patriarchal line of God's people runs through the shepherd's fields.

Before we cast off the shepherds of the first century as unclean and untrustworthy sub-humans, we must affirm that shepherds were a critical part of the sacrificial system, providing care for the lambs that later served as offerings for the people of Israel. Some have suggested that due to the proximity of the shepherds of Luke 2 to Bethlehem and Jerusalem, the shepherds may have been keeping watch over sheep that would be used in temple sacrifices. Some have even gone so far as to suggest that a lamb deemed worthy of being sacrificed would have been wrapped carefully and set aside from the other sheep in a manger as to avoid any damage from the other sheep, ensuring an unblemished offering. This is obviously a significant foreshadowing of the role of Jesus as the Lamb of God who takes away the sins of the world.

The shepherds of the New Testament were willing to get their hands dirty to ensure mankind's ability to approach God. Jesus was willing to come to a humble and dirty place, becoming like you and me, to enable us to approach the Father. Jesus, taking on the role of the Shepherd, helps us to redeem the image of the New Testament shepherd.

There are significant shepherd references that should be noted in the New Testament. In Matthew 2, Herod's priests and teachers quote the prophet Micah in response to questions about the location of the Messiah's birth: "And you, O Bethlehem in the land of Judah, are not least among the ruling cities of Judah, for a ruler will come from you who will be the shepherd for my people Israel."[7] Matthew 9 notes Jesus' compassion for the crowds that sought after Him for healing. He likened them to sheep without a shepherd. Matthew 25 pictures Jesus as the Shepherd who will separate the sheep and goats at the time of Jesus' glory. As we have already noted, Luke tells the story of the shepherds who witnessed Jesus' early days. In John 10, Jesus draws the contrast between Himself as the Good Shepherd and the pharisees who care nothing about the sheep and run away. Later in this chapter, Jesus signals His mission in saying, "I lay down my life for the sheep."[8] In the Book of Hebrews, the beautiful benediction prayer calls Jesus the "Great Shepherd of the Sheep."[9]

Additionally, the Book of Revelation portrays a vision of the Lamb, Jesus, becoming the Shepherd of those who have come through great tribulation.[10] First Peter even explores the ecclesiastical roles and responsibilities of church elders as shepherds, and highlights their relationship to Christ as the Chief Shepherd.

While it is simply impossible to explore the incredible trove of the shepherd motif throughout all the New Testament in this book, it is important to understand that the shepherd image is a central part of the gospels and is beautifully employed by the epistles. As you will note in the chapters that follow, some of these themes will serve as helpful illustrative support to what we will uncover in our exploration of Psalm 23.

Pause for Reflection

- What does it mean to you that Jesus is the Good Shepherd?

- Read Matthew 2:3-6. What was King Herod's reaction to the prophecy that the Shepherd would come out of Bethlehem?

CHAPTER 3

THE ROLES OF THE SHEPHERD

"Want to change your life? Begin by saying, 'The Lord is my shepherd.'" –Max Lucado

What does a shepherd do? A shepherd looks after sheep. From a distance, that's all that is necessary to know. However, like a great many other occupations and pursuits, there is much more complexity to discover as we take a closer look. While we might say a teacher teaches or a painter paints, that only conveys the lowest common denominator and most simplistic characterization of the endeavor. It fails to capture what the teacher or painter really does. For example, a teacher who works with special needs students approaches teaching differently than a teacher with a group of adult online learners. Consider the painters. One might paint portraits, and therefore approach painting differently than the painter who colors the columns of a suspension bridge. When I was serving as a corps officer in the northeast corner of South Dakota, there was a very generous donor who was also a well-known wildlife artist, and a grand museum in the community held many of his original paintings. One Christmas season, I was planning a visit to his home to thank him for supporting the work of the Army. When I called to ensure that he was available for my visit, his reply was, "I'm just painting." The response did not seem sufficient for what he was doing. He was creating a masterpiece with unmatched skill and detail. "Just painting" was technically correct but failed to capture the larger context of the creativity and skill involved in what he was doing. The same is true of shepherding. To say that someone is a shepherd does not capture the full breadth of what they do. We have a notion of what it entails, but our concept is colored by our own experiences and biases. I understand that growing up in the Midwest of the United States impacts my interpretation of Scripture. This is also true when I think of a shepherd. It requires good interpretation skills and an ability to take on another perspective to gain a vision of the kind of shepherd that David is writing about.

Shepherding today in the Midwest prairie is far different than it was in the first century on the Bethlehem countryside. The twenty-first century sheep producer is encouraged to monitor the location and movement of their sheep using RFID tags and check on them with remote cameras from a smart phone. This would have looked much more like witchcraft than shepherding to first-century eyes. As we consider the role of shepherds, we will try to understand it as David would have.

I suggest to you that there are three primary roles of a shepherd. Those roles are provider, protector, and physician. Sheep have a deep dependency on their shepherd. The provision for the sheep under the shepherd's care is one of the shepherd's most crucial roles. They concern themselves with knowing where the best grazing pastures and sources of clean water for the sheep to drink are. The staples of life provided to the sheep depend on the shepherd's understanding of the land and resources available. The second role is that of protector. Sheep have very limited natural defenses. They are not able to dig holes like prairie dogs to escape predators. They are not able to take flight like birds to escape something that wants to eat them. They are not able to reproduce in mass numbers like rabbits to strengthen the size of the warren. The best and most reliable defense for sheep is the shepherd. The shepherd is the defender of the sheep, willing to risk his own life for the lives of the sheep. The third role of the shepherd is that of physician. The first-century shepherd did not have the luxury of calling up a local vet to come and treat a sick or injured sheep. Therefore, the role of physician, particularly in the ancient Near Eastern model, fell to the shepherd.

As we look deeper into Psalm 23, we will take time to reflect on the three key roles of the shepherd. We will also draw certain parallels from the psalm's shepherd to our relationship with the Lord, who is *our* Shepherd. I trust that this chapter has helped you to understand the significance of the image of the shepherd employed by the psalmist to describe the Lord. While I have chosen to give attention to these particular areas, I also want to acknowledge that others have offered suggestions in describing the role of the shepherd as well, particularly the pastoral role of shepherds in the church context. Commissioner Phil Needham has summarized one book's thoughts of shepherding ministry in saying that, "The shepherding ministry of the Church, passed on from the first century to the present, can be summarily described by four functions: healing, sustaining, guiding, and reconciling."[11] This provides a wonderfully simple pattern for the shepherd.

Considering the fourth role of the shepherd, reconciliation (suggested by Needham), I have chosen to group the roles of healing and reconciling together under the combined role of physician. In this sense, reconciliation results as a part of God's redemptive healing process. This is to say that as the shepherd participates in the ministry or role of healing, a part of that healing is reconciliation. This action of reconciliation can be seen throughout Scripture primarily as the reconciliation of mankind to the divine, of people to one another, and finally, of creation to the Creator.

Pause for Reflection

- What role of the Shepherd—provider, protector, or physician—is most meaningful to you in the current season of your life?

PROVIDER

There is a tremendous amount of pressure on those who undertake the responsibility of a provider. Perhaps you have some familiarity with that pressure as a parent, spouse, or person responsible for an aging parent. To know that there is another life dependent on you can be a sobering and unsettling reality. This is not to say that being a provider is not also richly rewarding—knowing that you are able to provide for someone else is a good feeling, too—but the higher the stakes, the more pressure the provider feels.

While the role of provider is clear from the characterization of the Lord as a shepherd, there are some who have suggested that Psalm 23 is largely about God's provision. Craig C. Boyles in his commentary on the Psalms has said that "most commentators perceive two images in this psalm: Yahweh as shepherd and as host at the temple. In both roles, Yahweh provides nourishment and safe passage."[12] One might argue that the Psalter is a tributary book that celebrates the Lord's provision. From the early chapters of the Psalms, the Lord is credited as the shield and lifter of David's head. The closing psalm acclaims the Lord's mighty deeds and greatness. David's depiction of the Lord as the Shepherd who provides is congruent with the larger theme of the Psalms. The image of YHWH as provider for all of creation resonates throughout the Psalm.

The role of provider is a part of God's nature, indelibly stamped onto the human soul. The provisional posture of God is a critical part of His image in which humanity is created. We are created with a sacred instinct to provide for those who are important to us. Unfortunately, that image has been flawed by sin and distorted by our own selfish desires. But it still finds ways to break through the hard shell of humanity's sinfulness and finds a way to shine through. Jesus references this human reflection of God's care and provision during the Sermon on the Mount, "You parents—if your children ask for a loaf of bread, do you give them a stone instead? Or if they ask for a fish, do you give them a snake? Of course not! So if you sinful people know how to give good gifts to your children, how much more will your heavenly Father give good gifts to those who ask him?"[13] Even though we are misshaped by the ravages of a sinful world, we know how to give good gifts. God has placed in every human a deep desire to provide for others. For some this desire has laid dormant for years, and for others, it is readily expressed in their daily lives. Still, all of us have this God-placed desire stamped on our nature. The desire to provide reflects the goodness of God in this world. It is seen in a parents' love for their children, a husband's love for his wife, a child's playful provision for their doll, the actions of those who work for the justice and care of those in their communities, and in those who work in the social sector or medical fields.

When humans take on the role of provider, their weaknesses are exposed and they quickly discover their limits. This was certainly true in my experience. I can still remember the day of my wedding, for all the obvious reasons, but also because of the overwhelming sense of responsibility I felt. My wife already had two small children when we were married, which meant that I went from being a single man with limited responsibilities to part of a family of four in one afternoon. My level of responsibility skyrocketed as a result of quickly becoming both a husband and father. It took some time and maturing to realize that the provision for this newly formed family was not only on my shoulders. My wife and I had remarkably helpful families who were very good to us and nurtured us along the way. In addition, as believers, we had the Good Shepherd as our constant provider and a wonderful church body who supported us as a new couple. We were able to often give testimony to how God had provided just the right thing at just the right time. Even with all the support and guidance I received as a young father and husband, I was still humbled in my role. Some of God's provision I recognized right away, but in other areas, I only recognized Him after time and my maturity had developed.

 God's ability to provide has never been exceeded by our needs, regardless of how insurmountable they may seem to us at the time that we are facing them. The Lord's capacity to provide is marvelously limitless. Mankind has the perfect provider in the Lord. This is what the writer of Psalm 23 is declaring when he says that the Lord is his Shepherd. There are other images that David could have used to illustrate the provision of God. The shepherd is a remarkably good illustration, and I am happy that he chose it. In calling the Lord his shepherd, David recognizes the Lord as his primary source for provision. Sheep do not have a host of providers from which they can choose from. The shepherd is their single point of provision and care.

David would have drawn inspirations from the old stories of God's provision for the patriarchs as he considered the Shepherd-King's provision. One of the stories that likely would have been recalled was that of the Lord's provision for Abraham. As David was taught the principal of the Lord's provision for Israel, and even Jesse's family, the story of God's provision for Abraham would have been a central part of his teaching "curriculum." David would have been prompted to imagine the wonderful relief and joy that Abraham must have felt when he realized God's provision atop Mount Moriah.

MOUNT MORIAH

You probably know the story well. Abraham's life serves as a continual testimony of God's provision, as he was promised a son and received one late in life. In addition to the seemingly improbable promise of gaining an heir at nearly one hundred years old, God also promised Abraham he would become the father of a nation. However, the most crucial provisional moment in Abraham's life might have come during the summit of Mount Moriah. It was there that the Lord's provision for Abraham would come to a crescendo. On the journey up to the mountain, the preparation he made in anticipation of what awaited him was devoid of any joy. He was heartbroken and filled with dread because God had made an impossible request of Abraham.

When Abraham was very old, he was blessed to have his son Isaac. To say that this child was a "miracle child" would be an understatement, but this amazing blessing was cut short when God asked Abraham to do the unthinkable: "Take your son, your only son—yes, Isaac, whom you love so much—and go to the land of Moriah. Go and sacrifice him as a burnt offering on one of the mountains, which I will show you."[14] As Abraham's old and tired legs carried him up the mountain, he comforted his inquisitive son (and perhaps himself) with faith and assurance that *God would provide* for that day's sacrifice.

These three words became Abraham's mantra during the climb to the summit of the mountain. God. Will. Provide. For Abraham, it was both a proclamation and a plea. The words were equal parts an affirmation of Abraham's faith in the Lord and a cry of desperation. The writer of Hebrews helps us to envision how Abraham's faith in the Lord's provision carried him up to the mountain top altar. "It was by faith that Abraham offered Isaac as a sacrifice when God was testing him. Abraham, who had received God's promises, was ready to sacrifice his only son, Isaac, even though God had told him, 'Isaac is the son through whom your descendants will be counted'" (Hebrews 11:17-19). Abraham reasoned that if Isaac died, God was able to bring him back to life again. And in a sense, Abraham did receive his son back from the dead."[15] It was Abraham's faith in the Lord's provision that enabled him to journey to the altar with his son in one hand and a cruel dagger in the other. It was his desperation that kept his ears open to the Lord's voice of intervention. In one nail-biting instant, God made good on His provision with a heavenly voice and a well-placed ram, which had such a profound impact on Abraham that he named the piece of ground they were on The Lord Will Provide.[16] Abraham could never again look at that mountain without remembering God's provision. The Lord provided in that moment what Abraham needed more than anything else in the world. The Great Shepherd guided a ram to the precise spot where he was needed.

There are several key lessons we can take away from this story related to the Lord's provision. Let's consider some of them now.

Deeper understanding of provision. Abraham was able to provide assurance to Isaac that the Lord would provide because he had a broader perspective. He had experienced the Lord's provision on many occasions over his long life. Not the least of which was the birth of Isaac. As the writer of Hebrews contends, it was Abraham's faith in the Lord that sustained him as he faced the hardest test any father could face. Because Abraham trusted the Lord's provision in the past, he could now trust the Lord for the most extraordinary provision yet. He knew that even in this dark hour, he could completely trust the Lord's provision.

It is often in our most difficult moments that we must remind ourselves of the Lord's provision. We have to draw on the Lord's past interventions to strengthen our faith and trust Him for what we face today. The more that we receive, recognize, and experience the Lord's provision, the greater our capacity becomes to trust in that provision for the future. It depends on faith, expands our perspective, and helps us to place our trust in the Lord. Had Abraham not been a witness to the Lord's provision in the past, it would have been improbable for him to trust in this extraordinary moment and obey the Lord's request.

We may not be able to fully appreciate God's provision in the early stages of the journey. After all, the first steps of any journey of faith can be the most challenging. While Abraham trusted in the Lord's provision, those first steps with Isaac toward the mountain must have been the hardest ones. Abraham knew that the Lord would provide, but it must have been gut wrenching to lead his son toward the mountain. But at some point along the journey, Abraham was able to verbalize that which he knew in his heart—the Lord will provide. Finally, at the top of Mount Moriah, Abraham was able to visualize the Lord's provision in the form of a ram.

That same progression can be true in our lives. Trusting in the Lord's provision begins as an internal matter of the heart. Intrinsically, our hearts know that the Lord is worthy of our trust. Those seeds of trust, sown in the soil of our hearts, grow into affirmations of faith that escape into the air as words. They become prayers, hymns, and testimonies of the incredible provision of the Shepherd. We begin to verbalize that which our hearts already know. The Lord will provide. It is both joyous and overwhelming, but only then can we fully exhale and embrace the Lord's provision. Abraham did not fully understand how the Lord was going to provide until he came face to face with the ram.

Pause for Reflection

- Do you have a Mount Moriah?

- Is there a place or a time that stands out to you as a testimony of God's provision in your life?

Perhaps you can recall a time when you wondered if God would, or even could, provide only to discover God was already intervening on your behalf. These serve as touchstones and reminders of God's divine provision.

Daily provision. Provision is cyclical; it involves both ongoing anticipation and remembrance. Mount Moriah was not the only singular moment of provision for Abraham and his son. It was a monument that could be recalled in order to muster strength and faith to trust God's *ongoing provision.* It would have been a reminder that the Lord was and is the Provider and Shepherd of Israel to generations that followed.

For the shepherd, being a provider is a daily occupation because sheep never cease to be in need. Much like sheep, our need for God's ongoing provision is a daily necessity, too. There are remarkable moments in which the Lord's provision is displayed, but sometimes God's provision is subtle. David declares God to be the ever-watchful provider in Psalm 121, saying, "Indeed, he who watches over Israel never slumbers or sleeps."[17] It is comforting to consider that our Shepherd never sleeps on the job. In Psalm 29, David exhorts Israel to rejoice because the Lord "reigns as king forever." God is the constant, eternal, and perfect provider for His people. In Psalm 23, David claims that the Lord is his Shepherd. In doing this, he recognized that the Lord is the ever vigilant provider of everything that Israel needs. We can have great confidence in this type of shepherd. We can fully rely on the Lord as our Provider knowing that He is always active, engaged, and purposeful.

Confidence in the Lord's continual provision is also captured in the second doctrine of The Salvation Army, as it affirms that the Lord is governing and preserving believers and all creation: "We believe that there is only one God, who is infinitely perfect, the Creator, Preserver, and Governor of all things, and who is the only proper object of religious worship." God did not spin creation into motion, then walk away to let its momentum carry it as far as it could go on its own. As Salvationists, we believe that God continues to preserve and govern His creation.

For Israel, there was no part of their daily existence unattributed to God's holy provision. In the Book of Deuteronomy, Moses lays out a series of potential blessings and curses for the people as they prepare to enter the promised land. The obedience of the people served as the crossroads between blessings and curses. In the list of blessings were all the things that God intended to provide to His chosen nation, and Israel was encouraged to recognize even the most basic of provisions as a blessing from God.

God's provision for Israel is extended through the priests who were appointed to minister to the people. David sees this and speaks about it in Psalm 121 in the same shepherd imagery of Psalm 23. In other parts of the Psalms, the writer recounts the shepherd's care for those appointed by the Lord: "You led your people along that road like a flock of sheep, with Moses and Aaron as their shepherds."[18] Take note here that David is affirming the Lord's provision and leading while acknowledging the participation of others, specifically Moses and Aaron, who serve as shepherds led and directed by the will of God. David is attributing the leadership of Moses and Aaron to God's provision. This shows up in the New Testament as well. In his letter to the Romans, Apostle Paul says, "Everyone must submit to governing authorities. For all authority comes from God, and those in positions of authority have been placed there by God."[19] One of the ways that the followers of the Lord were called to recognize God's continual and daily provision was in the celebration of the Old Testament sacred feasts. Each one served as a reminder of the Lord's provision.

The feasts are prescribed for Israel in the Old Testament, particularly in Exodus 23:10-19 and Leviticus 23:1-44. They serve as perpetual reminders of the Lord's provision and as a ceremonial way for Israel to remember the Lord and His care for them. The order laid out in the Book of Leviticus is as follows:

- The Passover, or *Pesach*, was a reminder of God's provision of the redemption of Israel from slavery in Egypt. During the carefully orchestrated feast, the participants recalled their deliverance from bondage and death. Each element of the feast celebrated and rehearsed God's provision for Israel.

- The feast of unleavened bread, or *Hag Hamatoz*, is related to Passover. It is a week-long ceremony observed by refraining from eating any bread with yeast. It was a reminder of the way in which Israel was quickly liberated from Egypt in haste, and of the suddenness in which God brought them out of Egypt. "For bread they baked flat cakes from the dough without yeast they had brought from Egypt. It was made without yeast because the people were driven out of Egypt in such a hurry that they had no time to prepare the bread or other food.[20]

- First Fruits, or *Yom Habikkurim*, is the recognition of God's provision of substance for His people. It recognizes the Lord's bounty in the promised land. It also recognizes the redemption of the first born in Egypt during the Passover.

- The Feast of Weeks, or *Shavuot*, is the joyful celebration of the Lord's provision of the Law after the crossing of the Red Sea. This is also closely connected with the celebration of the harvest, which also recognizes the provision of the Lord in providing for His people.

- Trumpets, or *Ros Hasgana*, is Israel's celebration of a new year. It was a hopeful occasion in which the nation looked forward to the Lord's coming provision in the new year. The people of Israel presented themselves before the Lord and sought His favor for themselves and for their families.

• Day of Atonement, or *Yom Kippur*, is a day of rest, fasting, and sacrifices, which serve as recognition of the Lord's provision in a system of atonement. It celebrates the Lord's cleansing of people, priests, and kings from their sins and purifies the Holy Place in the Temple.

• Tabernacles (Booths), or *Sukkoth*, is a celebration of God's presence. It recognizes the Lord's provision of the fruit harvest and is observed by families living in temporary shelters or tents. It memorializes the giving of the Tabernacle and the promise of the Lord's presence.

Provision of the eternal. The most critical provision extended to people from God through the priests was soteriological in nature. In Exodus 28, God sets apart Aaron and his sons to become priests for the nation of Israel. Their role, in large part, was to make an atonement for the sins of Israel, and in doing so provide assurance of God's salvation to individuals. The latter part of Exodus and a large part of the Book of Leviticus lay out the elaborate sacrificial system that would provide Israel a path to redemption and salvation. Timothy Laniak, who has given much thought to the biblical understanding of shepherding, has suggested that there is a strong connection between Israel's priesthood and the role of a shepherd. He once said, "The caring aspects of spiritual shepherding in Scripture are best exemplified in the roles of the priests."[21] It is easy to turn our thoughts to Jesus as we think about the overlap between the role of shepherd and priest. Jesus is the embodiment of the Lord's desire to provide for His people, to shepherd them, and to save them.

The writer of Hebrews offers good commentary on Jesus' role as priest for the people of God. Hebrews 10 specifically speaks to the sacrificial duties of the priests and its salvific effects: "... The priest stands and ministers before the altar day after day, offering the same sacrifices again and again, which can never take away sins. But our High Priest offered Himself to God as a single sacrifice for sins..."[22] There is no greater provision offered to humanity than that of salvation. It's the thing mankind is most desperate for; the one thing that human effort can never provide. Our dependency on God's provision is magnified by our inability to obtain salvation outside of Jesus as our Shepherd and Priest.

The Good Provider. The effectiveness of the shepherd can be measured by the ability to care for the sheep. The lives of the sheep that are poorly provided for stand in accusation to the failure of the shepherd. Conversely, sheep that are loved and well provided for are evidence of a good shepherd. As Paul reflects on the generosity of the church at Philippi, he makes a wonderful proclamation concerning God's provision: "And this same God who takes care of me will supply all your needs from his glorious riches, which have been given to us in Christ Jesus.[23] Paul is touting the ability of the Lord to provide everything that the church at Philippi needs.

When we agree with David in asserting that the Lord is our Shepherd, we also add our amen to David's understanding of the Lord as the perfect and perpetual Provider. If we were to take inventory of our lives and rehearse the provision of the Lord, we would have an infinite list of the ways in which God has provided for us. The list becomes exponentially longer when we consider the Lord's provision for all of creation. Perhaps you have a story of God's miraculous provision for you in a moment when you thought all was lost. You may have hundreds of smaller instances that link together to form a long chain that stands as testimony of the Shepherd's provision for you. When we take a step back from our lives and see the larger landscape of the Lord's provision, we discover that there is nothing in the universe completely independent of the Lord and His shepherd-care of it.

Celebration of provision. As we discover this, we find that from somewhere deep in our being we erupt with a blessing raised towards God. As Eugene Peterson has put it, "Lift up your praising hands to the Holy Place and bless GOD. Act your gratitude; pantomime your thanks; you will become that which you do."[24] Our gratitude for the Lord's provision is a cause for celebration, worship, and confession. Our lives should be a continual acknowledgement of the Lord's loving care. However, we often forget or just fall out of the practice of thanking the Lord for His marvelous care. This is why it is good when we gather and remember together the incredible shepherd-care of the Lord. Our prayer can be very short. We can borrow the four words that David uses to commence this psalm: "The Lord is my Shepherd."

One of the beautiful traditions of the Jewish faith involves rehearsing God's provision for Israel by remembering and ceremonially reenacting the Passover through an elaborate meal filled with symbolism and imagery. Traditionally, Israel would sing the *Dayenu*, a song that recalled the miraculous provision of the Lord during the exodus and celebrated God's care for Israel. "*Dayenu* ... loosely means 'it would have been enough.' In a traditional Jewish Seder, the Dayenu song is sung. The song goes through a number of interventions that God had provided the Jews during their release from Egypt saying if God had only done this … it would have been enough."²⁵ It is a beautiful celebration of God's provision and care. It rehearses Israel's exodus from Egypt and stands as a promise of God's ongoing provision to the hearer.

To rehearse the provision of the Lord in our lives is a good practice. As we think about the Lord being our Shepherd, it is natural to consider all the ways in which the Lord provides. In our Soldier Enrollment ceremony, we mention that during the enrollment of a new soldier, "each new soldier should testify."²⁶ This should be one of many testimonies given by soldiers because testifying to the provision of the Lord by a believer is an amazingly powerful part of worship.

I have a tremendous respect for colleague officers who are serving in situations that require an extra measure of faith in the Lord's ability to provide. It is one thing to understand the concept and quite another to have to live it out in your ministry. Many of us have heard the stories of our retired officers who served during times when there was no guarantee that they would receive an allowance. Some depended on the generosity of others just to have enough to eat. There are some who serve across the Army world even today where conditions are difficult, and resources are dangerously limited. For these valiant soldiers, depending on God's provision is a daily exercise of faith.

I can remember in the not-too-distant past leading a team of young people on a mission trip to South America. Our host officer was a joyful woman who was responsible for a school in a dusty corner of the Andean desert where it had not rained in over 125 years. Much of Peru is lush and forested, however, this region just south of the Peruvian Andes was desert. During the time we spent serving with her, we discovered that she had saved a month's worth of her very meager allowance to buy provisions for a special meal that she prepared for the team. This came at great sacrifice to her personally. I was proud of the teens who were a part of the team because after learning of her sacrifice, they pooled together some of the funds they planned to use for souvenirs, and instead, gave the funds to our host as a thank you for her wonderful care. She was overwhelmed by the gesture and thanked the Lord for His provision. Both she and the team members were tapping into the part of their soul that reflected God's character as a provider. Our host was willing to go to extraordinary lengths to provide a special meal for a group of young people, and the team wanted to provide for an officer who they admired and appreciated. It was also impossible to ignore that the collected funds the teenagers gathered were precisely the same amount as what their host officer had saved and spent on our delicious meal.

Another important part of a shepherd's provision for their sheep involves making sure that their care outlasts their lifetime. This is to say that a shepherd also cares for its sheep by training and empowering other shepherds who will continue to care for them. Think for a moment about the time when Jesus restored Peter following his denial of Jesus during the passion week. While restoring Peter was a loving act of provision, Jesus went further and repeated this charge: "He said to him the third time, 'Simon, son of John, do you love me?' Peter was grieved because he said to him the third time, 'Do you love me?' ... He said, 'Lord, you know everything. You know that I love you.' Jesus said, 'Feed my sheep.'"[27] While this is a story of redemption, it is also a story of provision. Jesus was entrusting the gospel mission to His closest followers. He understood the needs of His followers and that "the flock of believers cannot guide itself away from danger or toward lush pasturelands. Without human shepherds to protect and nurture the flock, the sheep inevitably will perish. Jesus' threefold command to Peter underscores the necessity of shepherds for the survival of the flock."[28] Peter becomes a human shepherd as many others will in accepting this calling from the Lord to provide for the sheep. As one commentary writer has concluded, "This provision of grace would be important, for the church would soon face great persecution and even church leaders would waver in their commitments.[29] Pastors join this shepherd ministry as they care for the Lord's sheep.

Lack of leadership comes up a lot in the congregations that I visit because much of the work of leading is placed on the shoulders of The Salvation Army's officers and pastors. They are extremely busy feeding the sheep. Many are feeling the strain of this enormous task and have little, if any, help. A lesson that I wish could be adopted from a shepherd's provision is the need to raise up *other* shepherds. If we fail to accomplish the making of new shepherds, the care and provision of the sheep will be limited to only our capacity.

Pause for Reflection:

- How is training new shepherds an expression of providing for the sheep?

- What is significant about Abraham naming the mountain peak, The Lord Will Provide?

PROTECTOR

When David wrote Psalm 23, I wonder if he thought back to his first job interview, recorded in 1 Samuel 17. The morning of that interview, David didn't even know he was looking for work. Why would he? He already had a job. He was a shepherd over his father's flock. Nonetheless, he found himself across from the king of Israel, being interviewed for a very dangerous job. In fact, it was so terrifying that he was the only applicant. After some time, the interviewer asked David about his qualifications. "Are you qualified to protect Israel from the fiercest danger it has faced in a generation?" In response to this interview question, David told a story... a shepherd's story. In Gene Edwards' book, *A Tale of Three Kings*, the writer dramatizes David's story from 1 Samuel 17. It is likely that the king had heard this story, which made David a folk hero back in Bethlehem. Edwards brings this already dramatic story into even sharper definition with his gift for writing:

> Once, while singing his lungs out to God, angels, sheep, and passing clouds, he spied a living enemy: a huge bear! He lunged forward. Both found themselves moving furiously toward the same small object, a lamb feeding at a table of rich, green grass. Youth and bear stopped halfway and whirled to face one another. Even as he instinctively reached into his pocket for a stone, the young man realized, "Why, I am not afraid." Meanwhile, brown lightning on mighty, furry legs charged at the shepherd with foaming madness. Impelled by the strength of youth, the young man married rock to leather, and soon a brook-smooth

pebble whined through the air to meet that charge. A few moments later, the man—not quite so young as a moment before—picked up the little lamb and said, "I am your shepherd, and God is mine."

The story illustrates four things to us. First, we live in a world that contains fierce dangers. Second, there is a shepherd who protects us. Third, the shepherd is up to the task. And finally, the shepherd calls us into action.

Fierce dangers. Some dangers are easily identified; they are the charging bears in our lives. They roar and storm and announce themselves with great fanfare. These dangers are terrifying but are instantly recognizable. Bears are brutes. They rely on overwhelming their victims with power and ferocity. Their attacks disorient and stun their prey. These attacks are a melee of barrages, each one potentially fatal. You may be acquainted with some of these bears. They say things like, "You have cancer," "I want a divorce," or "Your position has been eliminated." These days, there are a great many bears who snort and growl in the woods of social media.

In the work that we have been called to do in The Salvation Army, we encounter men and women who have been pummeled by the bears of this world: poverty, addiction, abuse, and illness. They come to our doors seeking assistance after being mauled by the cruelty of life and battered by hardships that would devastate even the strongest among us. I am grateful for those who serve on the frontlines of the Army's social services ministries and hear these stories firsthand. I believe with all my heart that the Lord has called and equipped the Army to serve those who know well the dangers of this world. The Salvation Army has its origin in what was arguably, one of the most spiritually dangerous areas in the world during the nineteenth century: the East End of London. This is the way that William Booth described the conditions of the East End as he was considering how he might get involved and make a difference in the lives of those who were suffering in great poverty and sin:

> "I saw multitudes of my fellow-creatures not only without God and hope but sunk in the most desperate forms of wickedness and misery that can be conceived. I went out and looked on the wretched sons and daughters of debauchery, vice, and crime who were all about me. The drunkenness, and harlotry, and pauperism, and slumdom, and blasphemy, and infidelity of these crowds had a fascination for me ... I not only saw but compassionated the people sunk in the sin and wretchedness that I beheld, and the everlasting woe that I knew must follow."[30]

It would not have been difficult to convince Booth that there were fierce dangers in the world at that time. He bore firsthand witness to the misery and poverty of a famously difficult generation. They affected Booth deeply. His response to what he witnessed among the suffering of the masses continues to inform the mission of The Salvation Army today: to preach the gospel of Jesus Christ and to serve human suffering in His name without discrimination. David recognized immediately that Israel was facing a particularly dangerous bear in Goliath. Booth recognized immediately that London, particularly the East End, was facing the bear of crippling poverty and sin.

You haven't forgotten about the lions, have you? It's easy to lose track of them. It is in their nature to be nearly invisible. They are equally as ferocious as the bears that lurk in the shadows of our hearts, but they use stealth and cunning to sneak up on us. Do not underestimate the lions of your life. They do not announce their attack. Instead, they quietly pounce. When we finally understand that we are under attack, it can be too late to mount a defense. You may have encountered a few lions over the course of your life as well—the betrayal of a trusted friend, low-grade jealousy, anger that lurks just below the surface. These are lions that threaten our peace and happiness. Remember the warnings of Peter in his first letter to the Church: "Be sober-minded; be watchful. Your adversary the devil prowls around like a roaring lion, seeking someone to devour."[31] Already in Peter's relatively short time of ministry had he faced his share of lions.

We as sheep face the dual threat of fierce dangers from both the outside and within. We are in desperate need of protection. Every generation faces both bears and lions. Moses' bears were Egypt and the pharaoh of his time. His lions were his own lack of self-confidence and the dissenters within the ranks of those he was called to lead. Samson had bears too: the Philistines. His lion was named Delilah. David faced down a bear named Goliath. His lion came near after he noticed a woman bathing on the rooftop of her house. Paul had the Roman bear. Peter had a lion who whispered to him, "Deny you even know who Jesus is." Even Jesus faced bears and lions. The bears who once shouted "Hosanna," had within a week growled "Crucify him!" Jesus told his lion, "Do what you are going to do quickly..." before he was betrayed with a kiss.

We all have a number of bears and lions in our lives. No one is exempt from bears and lions, and those who answer the call to ministry are certainly not immune. Some dangers are universal. The good news is that we have a shepherd who is able to protect us through them. David was able to fend off the lion and the bear. Our Shepherd is able to protect us from internal and external threats. Our Shepherd is more than able to protect us.

When David said, "The Lord is my Shepherd," he was testifying that the Lord is our ever-watchful Protector. Throughout the Psalms, the writers refer to the Lord's heroic protection of the weak. David affirms that the Lord is the "Father to the fatherless, defender of widows…"[32] In scripture, the writers (particularly of the Old Testament) use two groups of people to represent weakness and vulnerability: widows and orphans. They have no natural defenders or protectors. They are at the mercy of a harsh and unforgiving society too self-absorbed to take notice of the weak ones. The Lord Himself comes to their rescue. He stands guard around them to protect them from harm. They are His sheep, and He is their Shepherd. I love the picture that Isaiah paints of God hovering over the city of Jerusalem as its Protector: "Like birds hovering, so the LORD of hosts will protect Jerusalem; he will protect and deliver it; he will spare and rescue it." (Isaiah 31:5). One of my wife's favorite stories to share with children is *The Little Red Hen*. It is a story of the sacrifice that a hen makes to save her chicks from a wildfire. When the flames become inescapable, the hen covers her chicks with her wings, sparing their lives and losing hers in the same action. The story is inspired by the Lord's protection of His people. Because the Lord is our Shepherd, we have a mighty protector who ensures our safety.

BATTLE PLANS

We have a shepherd who knows just what to do when we

are under attack. When David walked into the chaos that had overtaken the Israelite camp in 1 Samuel 17, he found an army who had lost hope as their plans for battle had collapsed. David discovered that the army of Israel was facing a Philistine bear and instinctively knew what had to be done. You can hear it in his voice as he says, "Let no man's heart fail because of him. Your servant will go and fight with this Philistine."[33] I prefer the English Standard Version of this verse because other versions say things like, "Don't worry." In Hebrew, the words used seem to convey something more than worry. The word *na-fal* can be translated as "to fall, collapse, or be brought to ruin." Therefore, a very literal translation of this verse would be, "Let no human's heart collapse…" Why? Because the Lord has a plan.

When mankind faced its most dangerous enemy, our Shepherd knew what had to be done. We are given a glimpse of that moment in Luke's Gospel as he records Jesus' prayer on the Mount of Olives. Here, Jesus and His disciples are rehearsing the battle plans in the form of a prayer:

> Then, accompanied by the disciples, Jesus left the upstairs room and went as usual to the Mount of Olives. There he told them, "Pray that you will not give in to temptation." He walked away, about a stone's throw, and knelt down and prayed, "Father, if you are willing, please take this cup of suffering away from me. Yet I want your will to be done, not mine."[34]

Pause for Reflection:

- Do you know your bears—those things that are attacking your life?

♦ Are you aware of any lions crouching just behind you, ready to strike?

PHYSICIAN

The role of physician, or healer, is critical in shepherding. In ancient times, a shepherd was on their own in providing veterinary care to their sheep. Consider the remote nature of shepherding. Since caring for sheep happened in the wilderness, it was nearly impossible to provide care from a central location. The remote nature of caring for sheep, combined with the fact that there is little evidence to support the existence of organized or formal animal medicine during David's time of shepherding, suggests that David and his contemporaries needed to serve as primary medical personnel for their sheep.

Researchers have suggested that in both ancient Egypt and Israel, the earliest individuals to formally consider the health of animals were shepherds. "It is found from the Bible that the ancient Jews and Egyptians knew many forms of animal diseases. Moses established a system of meat inspection which is still practiced by the Jewish people in our modern packing houses."[35]

David, of course, was one of the most prolific biblical writers to discuss themes of shepherding. He was also the storied king and shepherd of Israel, and stood as an example of how metaphorical shepherds were to care for their flocks. The prophet Ezekiel was one of those writers who saw David as an archetype of the shepherd. In Ezekiel 34, he prophesied that the Lord would set up David, his servant, as shepherd. David had been dead for some 400 years as this prophecy was spoken, but what Ezekiel was actually pointing towards was the Messiah, who like David, would be a good shepherd to his people. Ezekiel 34 is also a good place to glean some valuable perspective regarding the shepherd as physician.

The writings of Ezekiel draw on the rich imagery of the shepherd to illustrate the prophet's commentary on Israel's leadership at the time. Ezekiel, much like David, calls on the image of the shepherd to illustrate the role of a leader in Ezekiel 34. He begins by leveling a charge against the appointed "shepherds" of Israel who have failed in healing God's people: "The weak you have not strengthened, the sick you have not healed, the injured you have not bound up … [and] you have not sought the lost."[36] Ezekiel notes that there are four critical areas of care that the shepherds are not accomplishing: strengthening, healing, binding up, and seeking the lost. Because of their neglect and mistreatment of God's sheep, the Lord intends to replace the insubordinate shepherds.

The good news for the people is that God, Himself, will become Israel's Shepherd and in doing so, search out His people. The Lord will go after them and bring them home. This was most likely a welcome message for the people of Israel, who were already displaced and living in Babylonian exile. In addition, the Lord says He will bind and bandage the people's injuries: "I myself will tend my sheep and give them a place to lie down in peace, says the Sovereign Lord. I will seek the lost, and I will bring back the strayed, and I will bind up the injured, and I will strengthen the weak…"[37] I desperately wish the church would take up its rightful mission to be the agents of the Lord and lovingly, like shepherds, bind up the injured and strengthen the weak. If there was ever a time when injured and weak people needed the Lord's healing presence in their lives, it is today.

I believe deeply that the Army could be a powerful arm of the church in this mission. Too often in the past I fear many of our well-intentioned programs have pacified a dying world rather than healed its deeply rooted ills. However, there is great hope as we venture into new avenues of service that take a deeper look at those we serve. The Army's Pathway of Hope initiative, which provides individualized services to families in need of employment, housing, and education while also seeking to address the root causes of poverty fits very well into this model of binding up the injured and healing the weak. We must remember that binding up and strengthening the weak is embedded in the DNA of The Salvation Army. As an organization, we must never lose sight of the fact that binding up and strengthening are spiritual exercises, ordinated and sanctioned by the Lord.

Seeking Lost Sheep

The idea of lost sheep comes up in the Bible all throughout Scripture, not only in reference to the exiled Israelites. In the Gospel of Luke, Jesus challenges a group of Pharisees to accept that God sees value in sinners (lost sheep); therefore, when a sinner turns their heart to God, there is reason to rejoice. Jesus famously employs a trilogy of successive parables to bring home this point throughout the rest of Luke 15.

The first of these parables, you guessed it ... is about a lost sheep—perhaps not exactly about a lost sheep, but more accurately about a *shepherd* who searches for his lost sheep. Each of these parables follows the same basic pattern:

> **Stage One:** There is something or someone who is lost. How they become lost (careless coin holder, curious sheep, or a son full of wanderlust) is irrelevant. What *is* important to know is that they are lost—hopelessly and

desperately lost.

Stage Two: There is a search that takes place. One search takes a shepherd on a wilderness trek. Another search is confined to a woman's home. The final search reaches only to the end of a father's property line. They are all searchers. Beautifully, they are all successful searchers. Joyfully, each of these frantic searchers are transformed into finders. Their efforts are not frustrated, which leads to the next stage.

Stage Three: What was lost is found. The sheep, the coin, and the son are all returned to the place where the searcher desires for them to be returned to. It is the place where they belong.

Stage Four: Elaborate celebrations take place to mark the happy occasion of that which is lost being found.

The Pharisees to whom these parables were directed recognized that sinners were lost. However, they were happy for the lost to remain lost. Their attitude regarding the sinners was worlds apart from God's posture of compassion and love for the lost. The Pharisees despised sinners and went to great lengths to avoid their company. They had a deeply warped sense of God's attitude toward sinners. As one commentary writer has said, "True to their name (Pharisee means "separate one"), they believed in separation from sinners because God obviously hated such people."[38] The implication of the Lord being the Shepherd of the sheep, including those who are lost, is that the lost are *worth* searching for. Because of their value in the kingdom, their return is worthy of being celebrated. This concept was absurd in the minds and hearts of the Pharisees. In the pious posture that the Pharisees adopted, the lostness of a sinner was a just and deserving punishment for one who had rebelled against God. Jesus' parables of the lost sheep, coin, and son were "designed to correct the error of the Pharisees, showing how God loves sinners and takes delight when a lost sinner is restored."[39] In God's economy, sinners are worth the effort of the search and the elaborate celebrations had when they are found.

It appears that the same misguided attitudes toward the lost were present some 600 years before Jesus spoke these parables to the Pharisees. In Ezekiel 34, the prophet condemns the leaders of the day who were called to be Israel's shepherds. Here is how he addresses the poor shepherds who are miserably failing at their duty:

> "Then this message came to me from the LORD: 'Son of man, prophesy against the shepherds, the leaders of Israel. Give them this message from the Sovereign LORD: What sorrow awaits you shepherds who feed yourselves instead of your flocks. Shouldn't shepherds feed their sheep? You drink the milk, wear the wool, and butcher the best animals, but you let your flocks starve. You have not taken care of the weak. You have not tended the sick or bound up the injured. You have not gone looking for those who have wandered away and are lost. Instead, you have ruled them with harshness and cruelty…'"[40]

Before we pass judgement on the Pharisees and their attitude toward lost sheep, perhaps we should examine our own attitudes. There is general agreement among believers that the lost are important to God and that we should hope for them to find their way to God. We would like to see ourselves as supporters of the idea that the lost should be found. However, Ezekiel is not only addressing attitude. He is also addressing engagement. Ezekiel's charge is that the shepherds were not searching for the lost sheep. God never searches for the lost in isolation. He engages the broader community in the search. He invites the faithful to join Him as fellow sheep-seekers. Ezekiel's prophetic words tell shepherds to engage in the search.

If you are a follower of Christ, by association you are a searcher. You are a shepherd with a mission to search after and care for lost sheep. There are at least three possible interpretations of Ezekiel's words on "seeking" or "looking for those who have wandered away." One theological dictionary helps us to consider the first two interpretations: "When used in a religious sense this word first denotes the 'seeking' of what is lost which is undertaken by the Son of Man with a view to saving it ... But the same term can also be used of the holy 'demand' of God who requires much from him to whom much is given."[41] God demands that those among the "found" be a part of the search party for others. The specific word used by Ezekiel has a wonderful third alternative translation. His word for "seeking" can also be translated into English to mean "conspire." That is, God invites His shepherds to conspire with Him to find lost sheep. God launched this great conspiracy to search for lost sheep and called us conspirators into this vital mission. This collection of conspirators is corporately known as the Church. You hear it in Christ's words to the disciples at His ascension:

"But you will receive power when the Holy Spirit comes upon you. And you will be my witnesses, telling people about me everywhere—in Jerusalem, throughout Judea, in Samaria, and to the ends of the earth."[42]

Jesus invited His first disciples to become fellow searchers. By association, we are also invited to become a part of the divine search party. The question for us is, are we engaged in this divine conspiracy to seek the lost? If we can adopt God's attitude towards the lost, then we can understand that every person who is lost is worth the search.

When we lose something, our feelings can range from frustration to sheer panic depending on what was lost. As the stakes grow larger, the emotions grow exponentially. Any parent who loses track of their child understands the intense panic and dread that quickly consumes you. Take a small news story involving the parents and grandparents of a three-year-old boy in North Carolina in early 2019. The boy was playing in the backyard of his great-grandparents' home when he suddenly went missing. As several days went by and the weather got colder, any hope of finding him alive seemed to be fading. But against all hope, the boy was found alive. The parents and grandparents have something in common with the searchers of Jesus' parables: they have found what they are looking for. The news of the boy was splashed across television screens, newspapers, and the internet for days after the successful search. Those who read the story joined in wonderful amazement that this toddler was found alive. And that same kind of celebration should be repeated again and again when lost sinners are found and restored to their Father and Shepherd.

Pause for Reflection

- Can you recall your feelings when you lost something precious? How did you react?

- What was your reaction when you located what you lost?

- What point was Jesus making in telling the Luke 15 parables?

CHAPTER 4
I SHALL NOT WANT

"And I will set up shepherds over them which shall feed them: and they shall fear no more, nor be dismayed, neither shall they be lacking, saith the LORD." –Jeremiah 23:4 (KJV)

This second phrase in Psalm 23 is an interesting one. Many translators of the Old Testament have chosen to translate the Hebrew verb *haser* to mean the English word "want." In the above verse, that verb is preceded by a negative marker as to place the verb in the negative. The verb itself is written in the first-person singular voice. When these are placed together, the subject (in this case, David) has a negative relationship to the verb in past, present, and future. The verb, as it is written, works for any of these tenses. Since Hebrew does not employ tenses the same way that English does, the translator must choose how to bring the phrase into English. Most have chosen something like "I shall not want." But of the twenty-three times that *haser* is used in the Old Testament, more than half the time it is translated as the words "to lack." Therefore, the last bit of this verse can literally be translated to mean, "I am not in a state of lacking."

What does it mean to lack or want?

Our understanding of wanting is heavily influenced by the modern culture in which we live. Today, wanting has much more to do with desire than with the notion of lacking. That is to say, much of twenty-first century marketing in the West is designed to appeal to our desires rather than to the most basic necessities of life. What do we think about when we consider the idea of wanting? Perhaps this illustration will help us to understand.

Once or twice a year I have an opportunity to catch up on the world of Saturday morning cartoons. My granddaughter and I get to spend some quality time together as we watch cartoons while we prepare a breakfast of waffles, eggs, and sausage. She is an expert at measuring out the right ingredients and mixing them into a creamy, smooth, golden batter, but I have noticed a phenomenon that takes place during each commercial break. My granddaughter is very focused on making sure the batter is perfect until the commercials come on. After each commercial featuring the latest new and exciting toy or game, she looks at me and says these four words: "Grandpa, I want that." I think this conveys, in an oversimplified way, our notion of the verb "to want." It is the desire to possess something that you currently do not have.

    This is a rather modern understanding of the concept of wanting. In thirteenth and fourteenth-century Europe, the concept was more closely aligned with the ancient Hebrew understanding. For example, the middle-English word "wanian" describes someone or something that is depraved or in a state of destitution. *The Dictionary of Hebrew Languages with Semantic Domains* has defined *ḥaser* (to want) this way: "to not have enough of what is needed."[43] Both the middle English and Hebrew concept of wanting has a much more desperate connotation than that of the more modern understanding of the verb.

    To help us gain more understanding of the Hebrew concept, let's look at how the verb is employed in other parts of Hebrew Scripture. When King Belshazzar's dinner party was interrupted by an anthropomorphic hand scratching out a message on his palace wall, it was more than an entertaining party trick for his guests. It was a serious indictment of the king's character.

I Shall Not Want

The message left behind on the wall was a series of words that the king desperately wanted interpreted. After exhausting all the intellect and ability of the Babylonian brain-trust, it fell to Daniel to provide the king with a translation of the mysterious writing. Daniel's translation is that "… [the king has] been weighed in the balances and found wanting."[44] King Belshazzar's state of wanting or lacking was an indication that he lacked what was necessary to lead. The king was being figuratively weighed against God's standard for leadership and lacked the weight that was required to balance the scales. The metaphor of the scale is one borrowed from commerce. "A payment was to meet a certain standard, so if it did not meet that standard, it was rejected as unacceptable. Belshazzar's moral and spiritual character did not measure up to the standard of God's righteousness, so he was rejected."[45] This is a sharp contrast to the proclamation that David makes in Psalm 23. Because the Lord is David's Shepherd, he is not found to be lacking. The difference between the two kings could not be any more remarkable. King Belshazzar, at the height of his popularity, was found by the Lord to be wanting. King David, during a low point of his reign, recognizes that he has been found in the sight of the Lord to not lack anything.

When David proclaims that he is not in a state of want, there are two important themes that are inferred. The first is character. Even in all of David's faults and missteps, he is the person who God created and designed him to be. This means that there is nothing lacking in David's character. It is the God-influenced and secured character of David that prompts Samuel to refer to David as a "man after [God's] own heart."[46] David's character is intact and seems to have withstood the Lord's measurement. This he owes to his relationship with the Shepherd. It is because of this relationship that he can confidently say that he is not spiritually depraved and wanting.

The second theme is provision. In affirming that he is not in want, David is also affirming that every need is satisfied by the Lord's provision. He is describing himself as a person who is completely and utterly content with his circumstances. There is nothing David lacks, nothing that he must have to sustain himself outside of what the Shepherd is supplying. This is a bold affirmation, a place where a great many of us would like to be. It is a place of total contentment in which one is entirely at peace, not lacking that which is necessary for basic happiness. What makes this statement even more remarkable is its large context. It is broadly accepted that Psalm 23 was written and "belongs to the time of the rebellion under Absalom."[47] It is during this time that David was exiled from his palace and forced to run for his life into the Judean desert alongside a few loyal followers. Based on the description given, it looks as if David is in a place of *severe* lacking or wanting—the desert lacked enough water to properly sustain life, enough shade from the overwhelming heat, all the comforts of home, and of course, the prestige of the palace in Jerusalem. However, it is here that David makes his great affirmation of God's provision.

Too often we tie our temporary circumstances to our worth. We embrace an identity that is based on our circumstances while ignoring the worth that is ours due to our relationship with the great Shepherd. When we face hard situations and resources seem to fall short, we can question God's care for us. In the darkest and most desperate moments, we must come to realize just how complete and real God's provision is.

Wanting nothing says as much about the Shepherd as it does

the sheep. David's affirmation is in direct connection with his relationship to the Shepherd-King. It is precisely because the Lord was David's Shepherd that David lacked nothing. A shepherd has the responsibility to provide for the sheep under his care. Sheep that are found to be wanting are a poor reflection on the ability of the shepherd. Shepherds must know where the sources of water are and where to graze the sheep. Even in the hot and unforgiving wilderness, the shepherd must know how to lead the sheep to the sources of substance. I can distinctly remember our guide taking us to a place she called David's Pool during our tour of Israel. As we walked along a gravel path through what appeared to be wilderness in every direction as far as the eye could see, we stopped for a moment and our guide asked us to survey the horizon. It was full of stark and endless, barren hills. She talked to us about the importance of knowing the land as a shepherd and knowing where the streams emerged from the hills. We marched over one final hill. In the shallow valley there was a natural pool fed by a waterfall and lots of young people swimming and enjoying the day. It was a welcome sight for our group as we made our way down to the water. We trusted our guide and she led us to a place of refreshment and joy.

When we understand that the Lord is our Shepherd and that He desires our wellbeing, we can lean into His provision. We can trust Him even when we find ourselves in the wilderness of disappointment and failure. We can trust His guidance when we have no idea where to turn. Even in those times, we like David, can affirm that because the Lord is our Shepherd, we lack nothing—we are not in a state of want. David Williams has captured this thought well in his commentary of this psalm. He wrote, "Every need will be met by the guiding, providing hand of God."[48] We can rest assured when we understand that God is our Shepherd and that we are under His watchful care. Because of God's generous provision, we have all that we need to sustain us. That does not mean that we will not face challenges, or that it will be easy, but God's care for us will sustain us.

This should give us a great deal of confidence in who we are in the Lord. We are a people who are cared and provided for by Him. We often look outside of that provision to determine our worth and value. We weigh and measure ourselves by standards that the Lord never intended us to measure ourselves by. As a result, we become very uncomfortable. There are three ways in which we most often allow these measures:

We Compare Ourselves to Other People.

Comparing ourselves to other people is an old and fruitless exercise. It is a shell game that lures us in and takes advantage of our nature. The outcome is fixed, and we can never win when we play the game of comparison. Comparison is a grifter intent on swindling us out of our God-given value. Sometimes he's there when we collect the best moments and brightest achievements of others and compare them to the areas of our lives where we feel the weakest and most humiliated. We weigh our worst selves against what we perceive to be the best in others. We ignore all the struggles they may be experiencing just below the surface. We wonder why others seem to have it all together when we are barely making it through the day. You can easily figure out what the outcome of this type of comparison is. We have lost before we ever begun. We find ourselves severely lacking and in want.

The grifter comes again when we ignore any fault that we might have and at the same time, exaggerate the faults of others. We cannot seem to resist this type of judgment. Jesus even addressed it in His Sermon on the Mount. He asked the question, "And why worry about a speck in your friend's eye when you have a log in your own?"[49] The answer is very simple: we have not understood how to measure our worth and value as the Lord has intended us to.

We Measure Ourselves By Our Own Expectations Even When They Are Absurdly Unrealistic.
As I am writing this chapter, it is still early in the year. This is the season when otherwise intelligent and rational adults set unrealistic expectations for themselves. They mask these unrealistic expectations in the simple phrase, "New Year's Resolutions." "Before the first month of the year has even come to an end, most people have given up on their annual commitment to themselves. Research conducted by Strava, the social network for athletes, has discovered that January 22, is the fateful day [when] New Year's resolutions [are jettisoned]."[50] Resist the strong pull to measure yourself by these unrealistic expectations. When we buy into this dangerous pattern of comparison, we feel like failures because we cannot achieve that which is unrealistic. Our reality can never compare to the idealistic storybook images we conjure up. If you are wise enough to reject the temptation of comparison, you can hear the Shepherd lovingly say to you that in Him you lack nothing.

We Measure Ourselves Against the Latest Invention of Culture.
This comparison is counterproductive and uselessly exerts energy in areas the Lord has not intended us to work. As ministry leaders, one of the most significant dangers to accomplishing all God intends for us to do in our present job or appointment involves comparing our jobs to *other* jobs or appointments.

During the appointment planning process for The Salvation Army, leaders are reminded not to share appointments that were discussed but not actually given with other officers. In part, this is because therein lies an irritable urge to compare that phantom appointment with reality. Many have been haunted in comparing what they have to that which never existed. Establishing a value with inaccurate measures is something that transcends our spiritual life; it also clearly intersects into the secular world. In a 2017 article entitled, "5 things That Shouldn't Determine Your Self-Worth (But Probably Do)", *Inc. Magazine* listed four ways by which you should never measure your self-worth: through your image, through your net worth, through what you do, and finally, through what you achieve.

Pause for Reflection

Read the following statements aloud:

+ I measure up.

+ I do not need to compare myself to others.

+ I am loved and accepted.

+ I have a Shepherd who will never fail.

Now go back and read them again…

CHAPTER 5

FOUR BLESSINGS

"From your lofty abode you water the mountains; the earth is satisfied with the fruit of your work. You cause the grass to grow for the livestock and plants for man to cultivate, that he may bring forth food from the earth" –Psalm 104:13-14.

*"He lets me rest in green meadows;
he leads me beside peaceful streams.
He renews my strength.
He guides me along right paths,
bringing honor to his name." –Psalm 23:2-3*

Psalm 23:2-3 can be seen as a set of four consecutive blessings, confessed by David and attributed to YHWH: Sabbath, peace, restoration, and presence. They should be seen as a group, but it's worth exploring how David understands and receives *each* of them. These blessings open with God's divine pattern of rest, or Sabbath, reflected by the imagery of sheep lying down in green pasture. The next blessing is one of peace, which David illustrates in the shepherd leading sheep to and along the blessing of quiet, restorative waters. The third blessing is one of restoration as David affirms that the Lord restores his soul. Finally, the concluding blessing comes in the way of an invitation to obedient holiness, to be led in the paths of righteousness. Together, the set of blessings conveys David's view of God's provision and care for him. Independently, they are powerful affirmations of God's love and care for Israel. Collectively, they inform mankind of God's divine grace. We learn of God's care and provision for all of mankind through these blessings as David recognizes them for himself and for God's chosen people.

The blessings in verses 2-3 reveal the nature of God, but also allow us to see the pattern of God's intention for His flock—the people of God. They help us discover how God intends for His followers to live their lives. God wants us to be a people who adopt healthy patterns of rest year-round. If fact, He is in the business of restoration, and the crowning restoration project in His portfolio is humanity. God has a desire for us to live holy lives guided by the path of righteousness that He carefully curates for us. He also desires for us to be in close relationship with Him and gives us the precious gift of His continual presence, even in the hardest moments of our lives.

SABBATH

He makes me lie down in green pastures.

Pastureland was and continues to be the primary source of sustenance for sheep and other livestock. Even in ultra-modern Western society, it is estimated by the USDA "that nearly half of the lower forty-eight states is grazing land: range, pasture, hay, and grazed forest."[51] An understanding of land management, conservation practices, and the ecological sciences is critical for healthy animals and sustainability of food sources for livestock.

When I hear the phrase, "green pastures," my mind's eye is influenced by 1970s television. More specifically, *Little House on the Prairie*. I can see the sun-drenched valley and Laura Ingalls Wilder racing down the gentle slope of waist-deep prairie grass. The air is littered with dragonflies and dandelions. I recognize that my interpretation of green pastures is compromised by my own culture and experiences, which is why it is important to carefully extricate David's words from our own filters and understand the perspective of the writer. During David's day, pastureland was both sparse and valuable. Some have estimated that the Palestine of Psalm 23 would have been approximately seventy percent desert. To lie down in green pastures represents God's extraordinary provision of life and nourishment to His people. David recognizes God's provision of life and nourishment as he affirms that it is the Lord who makes him lie down in this pleasant place. He equates God's care of Israel to that of a shepherd who brings his sheep to a pasture teeming with tender green plants. The sheep are welcome to eat to their hearts' content. We should not, however, overlook the importance of posture in this blessing. The writer has indicated that he is lying down, which is significant because sheep do not position themselves that way naturally. As one writer has said, "Sheep seldom lie down as they are restless creatures always searching for grass to munch or stressed about their surroundings. They are tender animals that are easily spooked and startled, for they are entirely defenseless against predators and nature."[52] Lying down conveys a sense of comfort, rest, safety, and contentment. It is one thing to wander and graze in green pastures, but it is another to settle in and peacefully hunker down without fear or anxiety, knowing that you are under the shepherd's watchful eye.

When we look closely at the verb *rar-bas*, meaning "to lie down," the word is written with a grammatical stem that indicates a causative action of subject (God) on the object (David). The Lord *causes* David to lie down. It is a stronger sense than that of being permissive. Nearly every textual comparison has translated this to mean "makes" or "causes." Although, the New Living Translation is a notable exception as it chooses to translate this verb to "lets." I would argue that this is a poor translation of the

Hebrew verb. The implication of the Hebrew verb in the way it has been written is that the Lord is causing the action. The Lord *makes* David lie down. Interestingly, this particular verb and its grammatical stem is used almost exclusively in the context of shepherds making sheep lie down. Apparently, sheep required some causative pressure to rest. Perhaps this was true of David. Perhaps it is true of us as well.

There are some who choose to soften the verb to present a God who is offering an invitation to lie down in green pastures. One recent article that reflects on this passage says, "God doesn't 'make' us lie down, but He offers His peace and contentment every day to those who seek it."[53] This is not what the Hebrew verb indicates. The purest translation of this verb indicates that God is making or forcing the writer to lie down. It should be noted that the writer is not protesting God's action. In fact, he counts it as a blessing. Remember, it is a part of a four-blessing set that David affirms as coming from God. David says that the Lord has caused him to lie down in a pleasant place of rest, comfort, and nourishment. Being made to lie down is not a bad thing. In fact, it fits into a larger pattern of God's design. We have been created with a need to stop, rest, and lie down. When we ignore that pattern, there are consequences. Just try to stay awake for long periods of time. Eventually your body will take over despite your desire to stay awake. Important functions begin to fail when we are sleep deprived. Why? Because God has designed a daily pattern of rest and sleep. He has also designed a larger pattern of work and rest, which we call Sabbath. God demonstrates this pattern in the creation narrative. As He paused from the mighty acts of creation, Genesis 2:2 notes that God "finished his work that he had done, and he rested on the seventh day from all his work that he had done." The pattern of stopping was given to the Israelites at Sinai—and by extension, the believers of today—as a part of the Ten Commandments. God making us lie down is a consistent thing for Him to do. The following are examples of God's direct intervention in stopping someone or something:

- The Lord stopped Saul dead in his tracks as he was on the way to Damascus (Acts 9).

- God made Ezekiel lie on his side for 390 days as a sign of God's discipline for Israel and Judah (Ezekiel 4).

- Timothy, Paul, and Silas were prevented by the Spirit from entering Mysia. (Acts 16).

- God stopped the sun in its path over the battlefield at Gibeon as Joshua defeated the Amorites (Joshua 10).

Why does God *cause* us to lie down rather than invite us to do so? It is because God knows us well. We tend to run non-stop. This is particularly true of the western world. Recent studies of both the United States and Europe have shown that people in the West are working longer and with more intensity than ever before. Yet despite adopting long hours and intense workdays, productivity has proven to be inferior. *Forbes Magazine* has noted that "unfortunately, using smart devices, working 24/7 and treating everything as a fire has brought about a work culture where we are working harder than ever—but not smarter."[54] This non-stop work has resulted in workers "missing out on the stress release, energy boost and social time that they need to function at the top of their game the next day at work."[55] The insanely busy world is beginning to discover what God has always known.

We need to lie down, rest, and recharge.

God may have already made you lie down in your life. Sometimes, it comes through God's direct intervention, but often what causes us to stop is the result of systems that God put into place. We reach the point of exhaustion or illness due to pushing ourselves too hard. We all know people who push themselves too far, and perhaps you are one of those people. If you know that you are among those who are hopelessly trapped in the buzz saw of business and nonstop production, close this book, take off your shoes, turn off your phone, find a comfortable spot, and take a nap. Ask God to make you lie down. You probably need it more than you even know. As I mentioned earlier in this book, lack of rest is a danger particularly prominent among those in ministry. On Rick Whitter's list of dangers for pastors, he too states that one of them is not having a plan for rest. He suggests that those who think of themselves as too important or too busy to practice Sabbath should remember that "[they] are not superhuman—the church survived without [them] for generations and, if necessary, can do so again."[56]

Pause for Reflection:

- When has the Lord caused you to stop?

- Why is it that we sometimes think of ourselves as too important or too busy to take a Sabbath?

- What are some of the benefits of practicing a rhythm of rest?

PEACE

He leads me beside still waters.

For eight years, my wife and I spent summers at a camp in the southeastern corner of Wisconsin. The camp was situated on a small lake built by the Army Corps of Engineers. While the name Army Lake makes perfect sense when you know the history, it's a happy coincidence that the lake is also home to a Salvation Army camp. The camp has a rustic charm and will always have a special place in my heart. One of my favorite features is how the sun sets over the lake. The waters are typically calm, and campers are treated nightly to an amazing display of God's stunning artwork as the clouds are painted with rich reds, blues, and purples by the sun, all reflected on the water below. Reflecting on this portion of Psalm 23, my mind took me back to this place and the still waters of the small lake. One wonders what picture flooded David's mind when he wrote about still waters.

The Hebrew words that David uses are wonderfully rich and have deep and diverse meanings. It will be helpful to unpack them a bit in order to understand the fuller and deeper implications of this second blessing. The word that David uses for what we typically would translate to mean "water" is *te'hom*. It can mean "water," "the sea," or sometimes even "to be filled to the top" or "flooded." As I write this now, Missouri and Illinois are in the longest sustained period of *te'hom* in history. The people in the southern parts of these two states are well acquainted with the concept of flooding. In the city of Minneapolis, where I now live, there is a major restoration project underway to restore what is known as the Owámni Falls. The word in the Dakota language means "troubled" or "falling water." The concept of *te'hom*, much like the Falls in Minneapolis, envisions this same sense of troubled, disturbed, flooded, or falling water.

The founder of The Salvation Army likened the conditions of the poor and needy in the East End of London to a raging flood that had overtaken them. William Booth saw the calling of The Salvation Army to join Jesus in a great rescue mission to save those who were drowning in the tumultuous waves of poverty, addiction, abuse, and neglect. The flood waters of poverty in Victorian England are mirrored in the ultra-modern landscapes of the American inner cities of today. A flood of opioid overdoses is drowning our precious young people. The waves of depression and mental illness are washing over people and knocking them off their feet. Natural disasters, homelessness, and hunger pound like angry waves threatening those who are barely hanging on. Marriages are slipping beneath the waves of infidelity, apathy, and disillusionment, never to rise again. It is in this turbulent world that the Lord offers peace.

The adjective that David uses, and that many have translated as "still," can also be translated to refer to a place where one experiences peace and rest from weariness. When these two concepts are combined ("troubled waters" and "stillness"), there is a magnificent sense of the Lord's power to bring calm into otherwise troubled situations. In a sense, the two Hebrew words can be translated as "the place where floodwaters find their rest" or "the place where the sea is at peace." If we adopt this broader meaning, it aligns beautifully with the mission that Booth understood God to be directing the Army towards. The Good Shepherd desires to bring those who are engulfed in the angry waves of life to the place where the floods are stilled, and the sea is quiet. The wise shepherds of the ancient Israel desert knew that the dry creek beds were peaceful in the dry season but could pose a serious threat to the sheep when the sudden and rare rains came. These creek beds, carved through the Middle Eastern desert landscape, could quickly fill with rushing waters that would easily carry away the sheep. Knowing the landscape, the shepherd could move the sheep to places where the water would pool in calm, peaceful ponds rather than sudden and dangerous rapids. God knows the wilderness places in our lives and seeks to guide us safely away from the floodwaters that threaten to overtake us. God knows the places where the sea is quieted, and the flood waters come to rest. He offers His steady hand of guidance to those places of peace. God is also still calling the Army to navigate the flood waters of poverty, hunger, disparity, and hopelessness with His promise of help. This call to join the rescue efforts can be heard in this song of the Army:

> Rescue the perishing, duty demands it; Strength for thy labor the Lord will provide; Back to the narrow way patiently win them; Tell the poor wanderer a Savior has died.[57]

Jesus' own disciples became firsthand witnesses to His ability to calm the sea. Jesus was drawing huge crowds of those who needed to be healed. So many people pressed in on Him because they were desperate for His intervention. Exhausted by this onslaught, He needed some space. He arranged for some respite with the disciples in the region of the Gadarenes. On the way, their boat was caught in a storm. Matthew records this frightening storm and Jesus' intervention:

> And when he got into the boat, his disciples followed him. And behold, there arose a great storm on the sea,

so that the boat was being swamped by the waves; but he was asleep. And they went and woke him, saying, "Save us, Lord; we are perishing." And he said to them, "Why are you afraid, O you of little faith?" Then he rose and rebuked the winds and the sea, and there was a great calm. And the men marveled, saying, "What sort of man is this, that even winds and sea obey him?" (Matt 8:23-27)

Still waters are also the places of cleansing. Shepherds could bathe both themselves as well as the sheep that they were responsible for in these calm waters. The wilderness is a dry and dusty place, so places of cleansing would have been a welcome blessing to a shepherd. There are few things as wonderful as being able to wash away the dirt and dust of the day with clean water. I can still remember being among a group of men who spent ten days on a mission trip to Valparaiso, Chile. We added a floor to a men's home The Salvation Army had operated for many years in the city. This was a significant construction project that involved doing concrete work, building block walls, and laying tile floors. One of the men, Steve, was cutting custom pieces from cinder blocks with a diamond blade grinder. By the end of the day, every inch of Steve was covered in ash-colored dust created by the grinder. His clothes, hands, and face were all one solid coat of cinder block dust. He was transformed into a golem-like character. At the end of the day, after the work was completed, Steve would look forward to a shower to cleanse the dust of the day's work and arrive at dinner as a new man, clean and refreshed.

William Booth drew on the concept of *te'hom* as he likened salvation from sin to a cleansing flood of restoration. In the third verse of "O Boundless Salvation," he writes, "My faith's growing bolder, delivered I'll be; I plunge 'neath the waters, they roll over me."[58] These "waters" that Booth describes cleanse us and set us at peace with the Father as delivered saints.

I am so grateful that we serve a God who calms the tumultuous waves of the sea and stills the troubled waters of our lives. I am also grateful that we are invited to come to the still waters of God's grace to receive His cleansing. We have a Shepherd who knows the terrain of our lives. He knows well the areas where we are tossed back and forth by the waves of this world. He also knows where the flood waters come to rest and offers the blessing of His guidance to these calm and pleasant places. He is our Shepherd who leads us to still waters.

Pause for Reflection:

- What are the troubled waters of your life?
- Where is your place of quiet and peace?

RESTORATION

He restores my soul.

This declaration of David's soul being restored by the Lord is the second of the four blessings captured in this passage. It is a central theme throughout Scripture that the Lord is the restorer of creation. In this case the Lord is the restorer of David's soul. One of the key tenants of missional theology states that it is the Lord's mission to restore all of creation. Psalm 23 agrees with that notion, albeit, from a very personal expression of it.

About the restorative nature of the Lord, Lesslie Newbigin has written, "Mission is the result of God's initiative, rooted in

God's purpose to restore and heal creation."[59] It is important to note that restoration is initiated by the Lord. God did not wait for humanity, or creation itself, to become worthy of being restored, but rather, made provision for a fallen world as a free and loving act from His own heart. One of the leading voices of the era was John Wesley. He was instrumental in forming the early thoughts on what would become the doctrine of Christian Perfection. He was also engaged in helping believers to recognize that there was great value in seeking after holiness, even if obtaining perfection was elusive. He once said, "The salvation which God wrought through his son should be seen as an attempt to restore the conditions which existed prior to human transgression. This can be called the restoration of Eden." This idea of restoration is at the very heart of the work of the Army and always has been. Bramwell Booth noted that "to restore them to the image of God means also to bring men to will what [God] wills. Thus, restored they will do his will on earth as it is done in heaven." In Harold Bagbie's history of the Booths, he notes that it was William Booth's conviction that having rescued the drowning man from the sea of misery, "manifestly the next thing to do was to restore him to life." Furthermore, in Luke 15, Jesus reveals the heart of the Father by noting that when a lost soul is restored, there is great joy in heaven.

    David identifies the Lord as the restorer of his soul because there is no one other than the Lord who can accomplish the task. It is the Lord alone, his Shepherd, who can restore his soul. This does not mean that we as humans don't try a great many things to restore our own souls. We are clever people who have incredibly rich imaginations. We employ a vast array of activities, thoughts, pursuits, ingenuity, and more in order to restore—or at least temporarily soothe—our troubled souls. What David came to understand is that we are powerless to restore our own souls.

One writer attempts to help us understand this principle by drawing insight from Psalm 23 and 42 as they speak to the condition of the human soul. In Psalm 42, the psalmist speaks to his own soul and asks why it is downcast. Phillip Keller explains that sheep who are "downcast" have fallen on their backs and are unable to stand up without assistance. He says a downcast "sheep is a very pathetic sight. Lying on its back, its feet in the air, it flails away frantically struggling to stand up, without success. Sometimes it will bleat a little for help, but generally it lies there lashing about in frightened frustration."[60] It is the shepherd that must intervene on behalf of the animal and restore it to an upright position. Because the Lord is David's Shepherd, his soul can be restored and put back on its feet.

Keller also explains that it is the debris, mud, and manure of the world that stick to sheep. They are "literally weighed down with [their] own wool."[61] There is ample opportunity in the world that we live in to be mired in all manner of debris. Like sheep, we are weighed down in such a way that we can be easily toppled. So heavy is the debris of this world that when we find ourselves flat on our back, like the pathetic sheep, we are powerless to right ourselves. It clings to us and hinders our progress. The good news is that we have a watchful shepherd who is ready to gently free us from the debris that has crippled us and set us back on the right path. It will not require a great deal of imagination for you to identify the mud and manure that you have had to wade through in your life, but it is important to remember that we benefit from a Shepherd who is able to wash all of the world's debris off and set us on our feet.

Pause for Reflection:

+ What weighs you down?

+ When has the Lord picked you up and restored you?

RIGHTEOUSNESS

He leads me in paths of righteousness.

David returns to the overt shepherd reference here. The reader can easily picture a shepherd leading a flock of sheep down a well-worn trail toward the pasture which will be their stopping point on the journey. This is the right path—a trusted one, well known by the shepherd and perhaps even to the sheep. Reflecting on his life, David would have recognized those right paths as ones the Lord led him to. There were times when Israel also closely followed God on those right paths. Maybe you are in one of those right-path seasons now, following the Shepherd closely. The challenge for those on the right path is that we can become complacent, find ourselves distracted, and even get bored. At times those paths feel well worn, and we feel constrained or limited. Like a child who explores their limits, we are tempted to edge a toe off the path. But the paths are there for a good reason. As Timothy Laniak notes, "In the familiar image of Psalm 23, the Divine Shepherd guides the psalmist on the right trails, on 'paths of righteousness.' These are the 'righteous ruts' or tracks that lead us safely out to pasture and safely home again."[62] Nonetheless, we are sometimes tempted to escape the predictability of those righteous ruts and blaze our own trail.

There are scores of examples of people who were on the right path but got diverted or distracted. King Saul, following a decisive victory over the Amalekite army, failed to commit to the destruction of all the land's animals as he was instructed to by the Lord. His failure was immediately addressed by Samuel the prophet in 1 Samuel 14. After the strong walls of Jericho miraculously collapsed, allowing Israel's troops to take the city, some of the people on the right path got distracted in Joshua 7, leading to disaster in their subsequent battle with the tiny town of Ai. Even David, despite all his mighty deeds, and his heart that aligned with God's own, got distracted and acted despicably in order to carry out an affair with Bathsheba, ultimately making her his wife through murderous means.

Since David knows firsthand just how easy it is to be knocked off the right path and distracted from following the Shepherd, he uses an unusual word for path in Psalm 23. The word he uses is one with military origins. The Hebrew word is *magal*, which means "a camp in a circle configuration for military defense."[63] David is saying that the Lord was leading him on the guarded paths of righteousness.

When we follow the Lord closely, He leads us on the path that He has chosen and secured for us. As a shepherd leads his sheep in the way that is safest and most beneficial for the sheep, so too does the Lord lead His followers. This does not mean there will not be any dangers, pitfalls, or distractions. Anyone who has followed the Lord long enough knows well that there are plenty of those. However, when we do follow the Lord, it is comforting to know that the path laid out for us is one that is guarded—even surrounded and encircled—as a barrier of protection around us.

The imagery that David uses in this verse is a wonderful picture of holiness—believers following the Lord's leadership along the guarded path laid out for them. We sometimes think about holiness in terms of a destination. We want to obtain an experience that transforms us into holy people. As we read through writings of the eighteenth century that were fundamental in the formation of the holiness movement of the next century, we can see that holiness was something the believers of the time desperately wanted to obtain. In an editorial, John Wesley once wrote, "Sir, have me excused. This is not 'according to Mr. Wesley.' I have told all the world I am not perfect; and yet you allow me to be a Methodist. I tell you flatly, I have not attained the character I draw. Will you pin it upon me...?"[64] It might be helpful to reflect on the imagery used by David to help us understand the nature of holiness. Rather than longing for some mystic, ethereal manifestation of perfection and finding ourselves frustrated in our efforts, we should consider holiness a journey in which we follow the Lord closely on the path He has marked out for us and guarded along the way.

There are many people who experience shame and disappointment because they have not been able to satisfy some self-conjured notion of behavior that they themselves have set as the standard of holiness. In her book, *Holiness*, Catherine Booth asks the question, "Why do hundreds of assemblies of God's people meet and pray, but nothing comes? They hold long meetings, and make long prayers, and sing, we are waiting for the fire...?"[65] She goes on to describe several individuals who are struggling with their attempts to claim the gift of holiness and suggests that they are all hindered in their pursuit. I have come to believe that many of those who are struggling toward the goal were, in fact, already on the path and following the Lord closely. Their desire and struggle toward holiness had become markers of that which they most earnestly wanted: holiness.

Like Wesley, they did not claim to have obtained it. However, I think God saw them as His holy ones who, like David, were on the path of righteousness. Paul in his letter to the Church in Philippi said it well:

> Not that I have already obtained this or am already perfect, but I press on to make it my own, because Christ Jesus has made me his own. Brothers, I do not consider that I have made it my own. But one thing I do: forgetting what lies behind and straining forward to what lies ahead, I press on toward the goal for the prize of the upward call of God in Christ Jesus (Philippians 3:12-14).

We are invited to take this journey, to receive guidance on the paths of righteousness. We are invited to follow the Lord closely on these paths. As was stated earlier, these are paths that are not always easy and free from dangers. Along the paths, there are ample opportunities for stumbling and falling. But take heart, we are still on the path.

Those who enjoy hiking can appreciate that great care has been given to mark out a path for hikers along the trail. Hikers also know well that there are reasons to be cautious, even on well-groomed trails. Hikers must watch out for the three R's while hiking: ruts, roots, and rocks. Thanks to these, very few hikers ever complete a trail without a stumble. The right equipment, a good guide, and lots of practice can help us, but the dangers are real.

This past summer, I took a run on a beautiful trail that courses its way along the shores of Beaver Lake in northwest Arkansas. The views were fantastic, and the trail was made up of crushed limestone. As I neared the end of the run, suddenly my foot caught a stump and in an instant, I was on my hands and knees. The very first thing I did was scan the area to see if anyone saw my stumble. I was spared public humiliation and was able to dust myself off and finish the run, but I took home with me a few scabs and scrapes as trophies.

Following the Lord on the paths of righteousness, we are also likely to have a few stumbles. I like very much what the Army's leading voice on holiness, Samuel Logan Brengle, has said about those who stumble along the way: "If Jesus loved him enough to die for him; if He still loves him enough to spare him, in spite of all his faults and sins, and to save him the moment he repents, trusts, and obeys, how dare we speak evil of him! And if he is a follower of Jesus and a child of God, even though he may be very imperfect, how dare we speak evil of him!"[66]

The nation of Israel was full of perpetual stumblers along the paths of righteousness. Abraham, Moses, and David all had their stumbles, but all followed the Lord closely on the paths of righteousness. You may have your share of stumbles, too. You might be right in the middle of a clumsy, YouTube-worthy stumble at the moment. Take heart, the Lord has a special place in His heart for those who seek to follow Him even though they stumble. Just ask David.

There are those who rather than stumbling along the path, simply wander off on their own. This is why the willingness to be led on the right path is so critical. It is remarkably easy for humans to stray off the path. Isaiah sees it as a universal problem. He laments that "all of us, like sheep, have strayed away..." (Isaiah 53). David's description of the "path" as a military circle encampment shows us that its strength resides from the outside in. The Lord guards the path and protects those on it from external harm. But tender and fragile sheep are strong enough to break ranks and wander off. As tender and frail as we might be as humans, our will is sufficiently strong enough to allow us to wander off into lostness. We are, as one song writer has put it, "prone to wander."[67] Some sheep wander slowly and move away from the path in nearly imperceptible increments. They have difficulty pointing to the moment that they began to wander. They just wake up one day and realize just how far they have gone astray. Others sprint away from the path with great speed toward the desires that draw them. I think of the prodigal son of Jesus' Luke 15 parable and Samson's Old Testament story as examples of those who sprinted off the trail. Whether at a sprint or at a crawl, the destination is the same: lostness.

The Lord's heart is particularly tender towards lost sheep. I am grateful for this. David gives a great sense of hope to all wandering sheep when he affirms that the Lord guides him on the paths of righteousness. As much as David wandered away from the right path sometimes, he was always only one step away from returning to the path of righteousness.

Pause for Reflection:

- What does it mean to you to be holy?

- How do you feel about having a Lord Shepherd able to keep us on the right path?

CHAPTER 6

Very Deep Shadows

"The remarkable thing about God is that when you fear God, you fear nothing else, whereas if you do not fear God, you fear everything else." –Oswald Chambers

"Even though I walk through the valley of the shadow of death, I will fear no evil, for you are with me…" (Psalm 23:4a, ESV). This verse of Psalm 23 is one of the most quotable sentences in Scripture. Chances are if you started the phrase, then someone could finish it for you. The danger with familiar passages is that we can read over them quickly and miss some of the nuances of those taken-for-granted sentences. There are several that you could quickly recite just now if you were pressed to do so. You could rattle them off with the cadence of a well-trained auctioneer. John 1:1 is one of those for me: "In the beginning the Word already existed. The Word was with God, and the Word was God."[68] What are some of your all-too-familiar verses? Peter Krol has said that one of the deceptive dangers in being overly familiar with Scripture is that familiarity "crowds out curiosity … [It] hardens hearts and deafens ears."[69] Let's not crowd out curiosity here. Instead, let's slow down and read the words again. This time, read them slowly and hear every word. Pause for a moment after each of the three remarkably powerful statements in this verse. Read and think about them as if this was the very first time doing so.

Even though I walk through the valley of the shadow of death…
When we read about the valley of the *shadow* of death, it brings to our minds the bleakest of places. Even as we read the words,

— 87 —

we can feel a heaviness in our spirits. One can imagine the deep darkness of a foreboding valley, the thick and putrid aroma that would accompany a place associated with death. This is not a place I would want to spend any amount of time. I wonder what David had in mind as he wrote down these words. What place or situation would have inspired his ominous word usage?

This deeply shadowed valley stands in sharp contrast to the sun-drenched green pastures and still waters of the earlier verses. This is a hard place, a cold place, an inhospitable landscape. The Hebrew word that David uses here, *salmawet*, can be translated to mean "deep shadow." One commentary writer has suggested that its literal translation is "very deep shadow."[70] There are other words that Old Testament writers have used to describe shadows. However, this word is used to describe the most intense sense of the word. As an example, in the Book of Job the writer captures Job's laments as he regrets even being born: "… I have only a few days left, so leave me alone, that I may have a moment of comfort before I leave—never to return— for the land of darkness and utter gloom [*salmawet*]. It is a land as dark as midnight, a land of gloom and confusion, where even the light is dark as midnight" (Job 10:21-22). Perhaps David is borrowing something of Job's heart-wrenching lament to help emphasize the most difficult and terrible of circumstances.

In other places of the Old Testament, less harsh words are employed to describe shadows. Isaiah often uses the word *sel* for shadow, which simply denotes shade or covering (Isaiah 30:3; 49:2; 51:16). This softer use of shadow is typically used to describe places of protection or rest. David also uses *sel* to speak of the shadow of the Lord's wings (Psalm 57:1; 63:7; 97:1).

Salmawet appears in the Old Testament a total of eighteen

times. Isaiah, Jeremiah, and Amos use it a total of seven times to describe a deep darkness. The Books of Psalms and Job use the word ten times. David, as well as the others, used this word to add emphasis to the extreme severity of a situation. It helped convey heightened intensity. It seems that in recent years we have faced a number of very deep shadows. A global pandemic, volatile economy, unrest, and anxiety have taken us into the valley of very deep shadows.

David was well acquainted with the deep shadows of life. He was born in a country ravaged by civil war. His brothers were conscripted into the king's army and he was expected to care for his father's flocks without their help. His sheep were attacked by wild animals that he then had to fend off. He was taken from his home and expected to entertain an erratic and violent king. He faced a giant in one-on-one combat. He was betrayed by both family and close advisors, and he lived under intense guilt for poor decisions he made as king.

David is drawing a parallel between the physical, foreboding landscape of valley so deep that its impenetrable to the light of the sun and intense difficulties, which are sometimes impenetrable to the light of hope. One writer has said that these deep valleys are "regions where there is no light, as if death had cast his dark and baleful shadow there."[71] No one likes to spend time in these places; however, this is where the path sometimes takes us.

David begins this verse with the word "although," which seems like such a gentle and benign word. However, a closer look at how it is used here makes it a bit more ominous. It is a marker of both emphasis and concession. David is affirming that he will walk through these deep shadows. Oh, how we wish the verse read, "if" we walk in the deep shadows, as if there was some hope of always navigating a safe path around the shadows of life. But the implication here is that we will each find ourselves in the deep shadow-covered valleys at times. It would be wonderful if being a follower of Jesus excluded times of walking through very deep shadows; if our devotion to the Lord exempted us from having to step foot on these painful paths. But this is false. Not only are followers of the Lord not exempt from walking through the very deep shadows, but the very deep shadows themselves are inescapable. Following the Lord will at some point lead us through those bleak, hard places. As S. J. Lennox has suggested, "The Shepherd may lead into the valley of the shadow of death, but this too is one of His right paths."[72]

This draws a connection between following the Lord Shepherd on the paths of righteousness and also following Him through very deep shadows. As one Christian blogger has put it, "The path through the valley is also one of the paths of righteousness in which God leads." While this is not a welcome thought, there is a saving grace. We do not walk through these very deep valleys alone. David provides us with the comforting assurance that the Lord is with us. He is with us on the paths of righteousness and with us even more closely as we walk through the very deep shadows.

There are three things to remember when you find yourself in times of very deep shadows:

MOVEMENT

David noted that he walks *through* the valley of the shadow of death. He moves. He hopes of emerging out of the long shadows of a present situation and returning to places flooded with light. Though he knows that he will have to spend time in the very deep shadows, he offers us the hope that this is not permanent.

When you find yourself engulfed in the deepest of shadows, keep moving. Do not give up hope and settle into despair. It is often just before we emerge from the shadows that the temptation is the greatest to give in to. I love the beautiful lyrics that Kurt Carr has written as an encouragement to believers who are ready to let go, "I almost gave up, I was right at the edge of a breakthrough, but I couldn't see it."[73] If you are in the valley now, know that if you keep moving forward, a breakthrough may be closer than you think. It must have been very tempting for David to give in to the misery and isolation he felt as he was banished from his home. Somehow, he was able to recognize that he could get through this with the presence and guidance of his Shepherd. Not only should we keep moving when we find ourselves in the deep shadows, but we should keep moving toward the sound of our Shepherd's voice. When our sight is obscured by the darkness that surrounds us, we must listen closely for the tender voice of the Lord Shepherd. He knows the way through this darkness.

It is important to note here that not all who find themselves in the deep shadows will emerge from the shadows unharmed. The promise is that God will be with you, not that He will help you escape the shadows unscathed. We recognize that there are some who have been called to these deep shadows and sacrifice much for the sake of the kingdom. I think of the disciple Stephen, who in the first century became the first Christian martyr, as noted in the Book of Acts. Though he did not escape the deep shadows of persecution, he did have the very real presence of Christ with him even at the height of his suffering:

"But Stephen, full of the Holy Spirit, gazed steadily

into heaven and saw the glory of God, and he saw Jesus standing in the place of honor at God's right hand. And he told them, 'Look, I see the heavens opened and the Son of Man standing in the place of honor at God's right hand!' Then they put their hands over their ears and began shouting. They rushed at him and dragged him out of the city and began to stone him. His accusers took off their coats and laid them at the feet of a young man named Saul. As they stoned him, Stephen prayed, 'Lord Jesus, receive my spirit.' He fell to his knees, shouting, "Lord, don't charge them with this sin!" And with that, he died."[74]

Stephen was able to walk through the valley of the shadow of death with supernatural confidence and reassurance because Christ was with him. Moments before he was killed, he was able to see the Father and the Son, who served as witnesses to his great sacrifice. When things were at their worst, he kept moving. He continued to preach the message that the Lord had placed on his heart. He did eventually emerge from the shadows. Just moments before he was martyred, the shadows gave way and the heavens opened. He emerged into the light of God's presence in glory.

A century ago, two single female Salvation Army officers served in a Canadian city plunged into the very deep shadows. One of the women was Captain Lillie May Hodge.[75] She served with another woman officer, a captain whose name has been lost to time. The city was in the throes of the Great Influenza epidemic outbreak of 1919. The two officers served their community faithfully and cared for the needs of women who worked at a local brothel. During their time serving in this community, the women of the brothel would often make fun of the two officers as they walked by the brothel on their *War Cry* selling route. During the crisis of the pandemic, the women of the brothel suffered the dual cruelty of a devastating illness and a community that turned its back on them because of their profession. These women had become very ill, and some had already begun dying as a result of the pandemic. Even the local priest refused, on moral grounds, to enter the brothel to perform last rites to the dying women. Thus, some women who once ridiculed the officers began asking them to come give last rites, instead (which was not a normal part of The Salvation Army ceremonies). Since one of the officers, Captain Hodge, played the guitar, it was determined that she would conduct the meeting at the corps while the other captain prayed with the dying and cared for women who were suffering from the flu. Understanding that this type of ministry could potentially be fatal, the captain mustered strength and bravely walked into the very deep shadows of this place, surrounded by death but also by the very real presence of the Lord. One can only imagine the beauty of the ministry that was given to the isolated and dying women in this brothel.

Captain Hodge's days spent in ministry to the women proved to be the last days of her life, as she contracted influenza and died. She walked through the valley of the shadow of death, but the Lord was with her and she with Him. Again, the promise is that He will be with us, not that we will emerge unharmed. It has been said of this captain that "compulsion, and an urging by the spirit to serve the lost took the unnamed captain into the brothel. It was her final service of grace and compassion."[76]

Mission

Consider the fact that the Lord is not only with us, but leading us through these very deep shadows. It is tempting to ask, "Why would the Lord lead me into these hard places?" The answer: because there is mission in the hard places. Samuel Logan Brengle once reflected on Christians hindered in their walk with the Lord because of their seeking more pleasant paths of service. He notes, "Like Peter on the Mount of Transfiguration, they say, 'Master, it is good for us to be here,' (Luke 9:33), not knowing that Jesus wants to lead them down into the valley to cast out devils."[77] Some of the most impactful ministry in the Army happens in places of very deep shadows. If you are finding yourself overwhelmed with difficulties, ask the Lord to show you His purpose and mission in this. Some of the hardest appointments I've ever served in now have a special place in my memory because they were places where the Lord was able to accomplish so much. There was mission in the hard places, and God had purpose in placing me in those situations. We are the benefactors of this amazing psalm because David spent time in the valley.

Muster

Deep shadows have the ability to induce great anxiety and fear. There are dangers associated with the shadows. However, because the Lord is with us, we can say along with David, "I will fear no evil." In Scripture, God's presence is closely associated with casting out fear. It was the promise given to Abraham (Genesis 15:1), Isaac (Genesis 26:24), Joshua (Joshua 1:9), and even to the New Testament disciples (Matthew 17:7-8). It is faith and reliance in our Lord Shepherd that helps us to muster the strength to pass the test of the deep valleys of life. "The person with a powerful confidence in Christ—the one who has proved by past experience that God is with him in adversity; the one who walks through life's dark valleys without fear, his head held high—is the one who in turn is a tower of strength and a source of inspiration to his companions."[78] The Lord Shepherd helps us muster the strength to endure the deep valleys, and our example to others helps them to also trust Him.

If the deep shadows that we experience are unavoidable, perhaps even a part of God's mission and calling upon our lives, then we can take heart knowing that He is with us. It is His presence that gives us the ability to keep moving, look for mission, and muster the strength to persevere. Accepting that deep shadows are an inevitable part of the human condition can prepare us so that we are not surprised or knocked off our feet when the shadows come. We can find steady comfort in the Shepherd who walks alongside us in these times.

Pause for Reflection

- Can you identify some of the very deep shadows you've had to walk through?

- What is important about knowing that the Lord is with us in these places?

CHAPTER 7
YOU ARE WITH ME

"To witness the perpetual marvel of the world's coming into being is to sense the presence of the Giver." –Abraham Joshua Heschel

One of my most important jobs as a grandfather was teaching my granddaughter how to ride her bike. After a bit of trial and error over the course of a week, she gained confidence and could balance herself without my hand steadying the bike. Still, I ran along with her as she wobbled down the bike path. As long as I was close enough for her to see me and know that I was there for her, she did great. If I was too far away, her confidence would fail, and she would lose control and veer off the path. Having someone close by was critical for her confidence.

David, the shepherd who would later be king of Israel, records in Psalm 23 how important and comforting it was to know that the Lord was with him. David confesses to the Lord: "You are with me" (23:4), and in doing so, shakes off fear, despair, and loneliness. One commentator has given voice to David's thoughts: "Though invisible, thou wilt attend me. I shall not go alone; I shall not be alone."[79] These four words attend David as he considers the hard reality of walking through very deep shadows. As deep and frightening as the valley may be, David will not have to endure its dangers alone. The Lord will be with him. David's short but powerful statement points to three critical aspects of the Lord: protection, peace, and permanence.

PROTECTION

The words David utters in Hebrew to express God's presence

are often translated as: "Though I walk through the valley of the shadow of death, I will fear no evil; For you are with me." The words "with me" can also be translated as "surrounds me." As a shepherd, David would have been exposed to threats, fears, and dangers while tending his flock alone day after day. Even in the very deep valley of the shadow of death, David exclaimed that he would fear no evil because the Lord was with him.

The presence of the Lord has the power to dispel fear even in the most frightening of circumstances. Like David, we can take comfort in knowing that we are under the Lord's protection. Fear only has power in the temporary realm of this world. The Lord's presence endures for all eternity.

Imagine the fear and anxiety that gripped the followers of Jesus after His crucifixion. A great evil had come upon the world. This small band of Jesus' followers had their world violently turned upside down. They were crippled by fear in the face of an evil so great that it murdered the Son of God. But the Lord sent a reassuring messenger of protection to the women who were duty-bound to care for Jesus' body. The Gospel of Mark records it this way: "Do not be alarmed. You seek Jesus of Nazareth, who was crucified. He has risen…" (16:6 NIV). In that moment, they discovered the fear-shattering presence of the resurrected Jesus. The evil of this world had not overcome the light. Without the presence of a shepherd, the sheep are a fearful, harassed, helpless, and lost flock. I am grateful that we have a Lord Shepherd who does not abandon His sheep, but instead is their continually present protector. Any sense of protection has its foundation in presence. A harassed sheep cannot say to a would-be attacker, "Do you know who my shepherd is?" and expect any reprieve if that shepherd is not present.

PEACE

Beyond protection, a present shepherd is a bringer of peace. David goes on to declare that the Lord's protection grants a deep and abiding peace. In the latter half of verse 4, David writes, "Your rod and staff, they comfort me." Some have suggested that just the sight of the staff assures sheep of the presence of the shepherd and brings a soothing peace to the flock. (We will consider these metaphors of the rod and the staff in the next chapter.) For David, the presence of his Lord Shepherd was a comforting assurance of the Lord's faithful care. David finds rest, peace, and comfort in the presence of the Lord.

Throughout the Psalms, there is a correlation between the presence of the Lord and peace. In Psalm 83:1, it reads, "O God, keep not thou silence: Hold not thy peace, and be not still, O God."[80] It is very much the presence of the Lord that gave Israel peace. He is the Lord who makes peace within their borders (Psalm 147:14). As Jewish worshipers made their way to the temple, and by association, into the presence of the Lord, they anticipated and prayed for peace. One of the psalms that was recited as the journey neared its culmination reads,

Pray for peace in Jerusalem.

May all who love this city prosper.

O Jerusalem, may there be peace within your walls

and prosperity in your palaces.

For the sake of my family and friends, I will say,

"May you have peace."

For the sake of the house of the LORD our God,

I will seek what is best for you, O Jerusalem.[81]

As a shepherd, David keenly understands that the peace of Israel, much like the peace of sheep, is only found in the presence of their shepherd. Anxiety and fear are constant companions of shepherd-less sheep because relaxation, repose, comfort, and joy are difficult to come by in the absence of peace.

PERMANENCE

The incredible thing about Psalm 23 is that it denotes permanence, something superior to the annual trek an ancient Israelite might take to a place of worship to experience a temporary presence of the Lord. Here, David conveys his desire to experience the *perpetual* presence of the Lord and all that being in the presence of the Lord brings. The certainty with which David composed Psalm 23 shows that he enjoyed an ongoing and permanent sense of the Lord's presence and peace, not a temporary or short-lived moment of solace. The Lord's promise of His presence extends into all eternity. As the writer of the Book of Hebrews points out, the Lord says, "I will never fail you. I will never abandon you."[82] The presence of the Lord is the one thing that this world cannot take away from us. Material possessions, status, and position will all eventually crumble away, but the presence of the Lord remains forever. It is this truth that cushioned the believers in the early church. This was the great triumph of Easter morning. Not even death itself could remove the believers from the presence of the Lord. Those who witnessed Jesus' resurrection understood, like David, that their desire to dwell in the presence of the Lord forever was possible because the Lord had made it so.

It is important to note that while the great Lord Shepherd

has made provision for His eternal presence, like sheep, we are prone to wander. The same David who desired to live in the house of the Lord (Psalm 23) and proclaimed the impossibility of escaping the Lord's presence (Psalm 139) also pleaded with the Lord due to his transgressions, asking that God not cast him out of His presence (Psalm 51). Our tendency to stray does not discount the eternal and permanent nature of the offer of the Lord's presence.

Psalm 23 is as relevant today as it was when David wrote it. We can enjoy the presence of the Lord today just as David did, just as those first believers who approached Jesus' tomb so desperately on that first Easter morning. The protection, peace, and permanence of the Lord is very much available in our world and in our lives. As anxieties, fears, and threats continue to rise, we can find great comfort in living lives that are constantly surrounded by the presence of our God who is with us. In light of this truth, it is right that we join our voices with others in the great anthem of The Salvation Army, proclaiming:

> Far across the field of battle
>
> Loud their holy war cry rang;
>
> Though at times they feared and faltered,
>
> Never once they ceased to sing:
>
> God is with us, God is with us,
>
> Christ our Lord shall reign as king![83]

It can be difficult to understand the implications of an eternal God and His desire for us to be in His presence eternally. Because we live in a world that is temporal, eternity seems awkwardly uncomfortable for us to grasp. It doesn't quite fit right, a bit like having your shoes on the wrong feet. One writer explains it this way, "God didn't create this temporal world to be our one and only dwelling place or to satisfy us fully. In other words, the here and now is not the end."[84] In connection to eternity, Danish philosopher Søren Kierkegaard reflected that the present is an abstraction of the eternal. That is to say, the present we live in is "the infinite vanishing."

It is remarkably comforting to know that God is "with us" from one broad horizon of our perspective to the other. But God's promise of His eternal presence transcends those horizons and extends beyond what any human mind can conceive. When David says, "You are with me," he acknowledges that the Lord is with him, perfectly in that moment in time, but also in a never-ending way. This concept is mentioned again in Psalm 139:7 when David asks, "Where can I go to escape your presence?" The omnipresence of the Lord is not only spatial, but temporal. The deep thinkers and theologians tried to understand the ramifications of this. They tried to help us understand it in terms like, "God's center is everywhere, while God's circumference is nowhere"[85] and "The moment is not properly an atom of time but an atom of eternity."[86] What the theologians have struggled to capture in a way that we can understand, David says clearly in four words: You are with me.

Because our Lord Shepherd is with us, we live under His protection, we enjoy His peace, and we are the benefactors of His eternal presence. It is true that we will have moments in our lives when we come under the harshest of attacks. There will be times when things seem less than peaceful in our lives. These are the trappings of temporary. They belong to a world that is fading away moment by moment. In the long view of eternity, these things will become less significant. They are what Paul calls "present sufferings," "nothing compared to the glory he will reveal to us later."[87] This view does not diminish the sufferings that we will face, nor does it mean the challenges we face will not demand our attention and sometimes obscure the eternal perspective. However, often after some time has passed, we place these sufferings in their proper perspective. The truth of Psalm 23 remains the same: He is with us.

Pause for Reflection

- Take a moment today and thank the Lord for His never-ending presence. Even if you find yourself in very deep shadows, know that the Lord Shepherd who was with David is also with you. How has the Lord protected you this week?

- How has the Lord given you peace?

- What does it mean to know that you have been invited to live in the presence of the Lord forever?

- What are some of the "present sufferings" that you can now place in proper perspective given the light of God's eternal presence?

CHAPTER 8

ROD AND STAFF

"Proclaim further: This is what the LORD Almighty says: 'My towns will again overflow with prosperity, and the LORD will again comfort Zion and choose Jerusalem.'" –Zechariah 1:17, NIV

David closes Psalm 23:4 with a reference to two iconic tools of the trade for shepherds: the rod and the staff. These became a source of comfort to David, even in the midst of very difficult circumstances. While these might seem like odd objects to imbue with this quality, David chose the rod and the staff of the shepherd to convey the Lord's comfort. These tools would have been especially familiar to David as a shepherd. They would have also been easily recognizable by David's contemporaries. Taking a closer look at each tool will help us appreciate how they strengthen the metaphor of God as the sovereign Lord Shepherd David employs in Psalm 23.

Because Davis is such a skilled writer, it is unlikely that the rod and staff mentioned are throw-away terms, or that they escaped his employment of metaphor. It is more likely that the rod and the staff were carefully chosen to further develop David's stance on the nature of God's character. (Although, it is worth mentioning that the rod and staff aren't a shepherd's *only* tools. One wonders at the obvious omission of the sling. We know from David's earlier exploits that the sling was a part of his arsenal. After all, the use of it against the Philistines advanced David as one of Israel's heroes in pages of folklore.) As we look carefully at these items and how they are referenced, we see that they provide us wonderful insights into the Lord Shepherd and those He calls His sheep.

THE ROD

The Hebrew word that David uses for "rod" is *sē-bēt* and has multiple possible translations. While not particularly exciting or intriguing, *sē-bēt* can be translated to mean "stick." It can also be used in reference to a timeline for a family or a people, similar to what we might call a "family tree." A rod or stick was standard for a shepherd's arsenal in the ancient Near East. In fact, it was the very first piece of equipment given to a child who aspired to become a shepherd. As the young shepherds mirrored their fathers and older siblings, they would dart this way and that with a stick in their hand, mimicking the movements of the adults. As the young shepherds matured, the stick became more elaborate and their skill with it would grow exponentially. We know that David would have had one of these sticks as he cared for his father's flocks and even when he made his trek to the frontlines to check in on his brothers. Remember the insults that Goliath hurled at the Israelite army as he sized up David in 1 Samuel 17: "Am I a dog that you come at me with sticks?"

The shepherd's rod, or stick, is described as a root stem with a bulb that can be used as a club or tomahawk-like weapon at one end of it. It can be launched with deadly accuracy. As a young shepherd, David might have even launched his rod at a lion or bear intent on attacking one of his sheep. Perhaps David pictured a rod whistling through the air and crashing into the head of his foes as he wrote the words of Psalm 3:7, "Arise, O Lord! Save me, O my God! For you strike all my enemies on the cheek; you break the teeth of the wicked." David drew comfort in knowing that like a shepherd, the Lord watched over him and kept his enemies at bay.

In addition to warding off attackers, the rod is also traditionally used as a tool of discipline for sheep. A quick toss of the rod can reroute a sheep from bolting for an opening in the sheep's pen. It can also be used to quickly break up a sheep scuffle. Neither the sheep nor the human welcomes discipline, and the writer of the Book of Proverbs understands this, offering his son words of wisdom concerning discipline: "My child, don't reject the LORD's discipline, and don't be upset when he corrects you. For the LORD corrects those he loves, just as a father corrects a child in whom he delights."[88] When a shepherd employs the rod in disciplining their sheep, it is not because they seek to harm them. They discipline to *protect* the sheep. They discipline out of love and care. This is also true of the shepherd who cares for sheep that belong to someone else, as that person is accountable to the owner for any harm or injury that the sheep incurs under their care. The owner does not want any harm to befall their sheep not only because they care for them, but also because the sheep are a source of revenue.

The Book of Hebrews recognizes the discomfort of discipline, but offers this advice, "For the moment all discipline seems painful rather than pleasant, but later it yields the peaceful fruit of righteousness to those who have been trained by it."[89] The rod of the shepherd is a tool of discipline, but a tool of care at the same time. Shepherds were careful to employ discipline to the sheep judiciously. The care of the sheep was of paramount importance for the shepherd. We can take to heart this concept as leaders and shepherds of others. There are some who have mistreated and abused those they were tasked to lead in the name of discipline. These instances are a distorted, broken, and evil misrepresentation of what is intended as godly discipline and should never be condoned under the banner of the Lord. My heart breaks for those who have suffered in this way, by the hands of those who have masked abuse in the name of discipline. It is critical for the church to adopt a strong system of accountability for those who lead. There is simply no place for these types of abuses to be tolerated within our ranks.

The Lord Shepherd disciplines us out of His care and His discipline is rooted in love. The sheep are of supreme value to the Lord Shepherd. If the Lord is your Shepherd, you are precious to Him and close to His heart. I am prayerful that you are able to receive the Lord's discipline in the manner in which it is intended—as an extension of God's love and care for you. It can be difficult to receive the Lord's discipline if we filter His intentions through our experience of past abuses, but you can have extreme confidence that your Lord Shepherd intends it for good.

In ancient Israel, the shepherd's rod was also used to count the sheep. The shepherd would hold the rod over the sheep as they passed in and out of the fold. This allowed the shepherd to keep track of the sheep and provided an opportunity for close inspection of each sheep. The Book of Ezekiel continues to provide further context for the motif of the shepherd. Ezekiel 20 says, "I will examine you carefully and hold you to the terms of the covenant."[90] This is what the Lord proclaimed to the displaced people of Israel as He prepared to call them out of exile to return home. One writer has noted that in the discipline of shepherding, shepherds would gather the sheep and make them "[pass] under the rod—a symbol of the Word of God—they would undergo a close scrutiny. The shepherd would run his rod backward or across the grain, as it were, of the wool. The rod separated the wool, allowing the shepherd to look down onto the sheep's skin. He was then able to see both the quality of the skin and of the wool."[91]

This connection to the Word of God indicates that as believers, we should undergo an examination of our lives based on the standards of the Word because it exposes the areas in which we are diverting from the path the Lord has laid out for us. It is important that those who follow the Lord regularly undergo periods of examination.

One final translation of *sē-bēt* is the word "scepter." It would be a bit unusual to see a shepherd in the Judean wilderness using a scepter to ward off threats. However, we must keep in mind that Psalm 23 employs metaphorical language. The Lord is both Shepherd and King. David's sense of the Lord's comfort was bolstered by the image of the stick-wielding shepherd and the scepter-wielding king. The rod served as a means of protection, as dispensed by the shepherd, and discipline, as dispensed by the King. David was keenly aware that the Lord's people needed both. As one writer has said, "The Messianic era is possible because of a fundamental principle understood in antiquity: protection and discipline breed security." The psalmist reflects this dynamic with poetic simplicity when he writes, "Your rod and staff, they comfort me."

Each of these understandings of the word "rod" can be helpful to us in our understanding of God as our Lord Shepherd. We know that the Messiah descended from the line, or "family tree," of David. We also understand that the Lord is our defender, protecting us from many dangers. We need the Lord's loving discipline to correct and redirect us from time to time. And finally, we can appreciate that the Lord is not only our Shepherd, but also our King.

SUPPER WITH THE SHEPHERD KING

Pause for Reflection

♦ Consider the different uses of the rod (protection, discipline, examination, etc.). What uses stand out to you as being a critical part of your faith journey? Why?

THE STAFF

The staff is perhaps the most recognizable and iconic tool employed by the shepherd. It is used to gently move sheep to where they should be. It can be used to knock down high branches to provide a meal for a hungry herd and is also useful for rescuing lambs who have found themselves in hard-to-reach or difficult spots. One of my favorite uses of the staff involves its use for aiding a weary shepherd in much need of rest. Several paintings, including nineteenth-century Swedish artist Gustaf Wilhelm Palm's "A Roman Shepherd," capture tired shepherds. The paintings depict the look of a man who is in desperate need of rest yet knows there is still much work to be done. He welcomes this brief respite, knowing that at any moment he will need to return to the tasks of the day. The shepherd places his full weight and trust on the staff. In my home each Christmas season, my wife and I set up a number of manger scenes. In one of the sets, there is a shepherd resting on his staff, much like the one captured in the paintings. When I look at that figurine and its posture, it reminds me that we can place our full rest on the Lord.

In the Book of Isaiah, the titular prophet records the demise of Jerusalem and captures the message from the king of Assyria, who chides them for placing trust in their neighbor Egypt rather than in the Lord: "Look, I know you are depending on Egypt, that splintered reed of a staff, which pierces the hand of anyone who leans on it! Such is Pharaoh king of Egypt to all who depend on him" (Isaiah 36:6 NIV). It stands as a sharp contrast between Egypt, who has been both friend and foe to Israel, and the unwavering reliability that David finds in the Lord.

Many today have been toppled because they placed their weight on splintered reeds. A few examples of false rods and staffs come to mind. Perhaps we trust in our jobs, our bank accounts, or our IRAs. Some trust in relationships and love. Some trust in their own talent and skills. Others lean heavily on addictions and substances. There are some who place their trust in political worldviews. David notes in Psalm 20 that some trust in horses and chariots. But when we place our trust in these splintered reeds, and they give way (as they certainly will), we find ourselves on the ground, bruised, disoriented, and full of painful splinters. We can, however, have full confidence and comfort in the Lord. His strong and unbreakable staff takes our full weight. We can lean into the Lord with a comfortable assurance that He will not be moved.

Pause for Reflection

- Take a few moments to thank the Lord for His unbreakable strength that sustains you. Name a specific time in which you had to lean on Him for strength.

CHAPTER 9

You Prepare a Table Before Me

"Small cheer and great welcome makes a merry feast." —William Shakespeare

As we reach Psalm 23:5, a major shift in the shepherd metaphor is employed. Up to this point, David has used the image of the shepherd to describe the Lord. Now, the fifth verse describes the image of a gracious host. Green pastures are replaced with a banquet table. Rather than reading of a shepherd who cares for sheep, we now notice a host preparing for a guest. There is no more wild and rough sheep pasture. Instead, there is a table, presumably owned by a welcoming host. While David does change his imagery, these two metaphors contain similarities. Both images involve care being given, sustenance being offered, and provision from the Lord. The imagery of the gracious host helps to provide insight into God's gracious nature and illustrates our invitation to receive the Lord's care at His table. Let's give some thought to this image.

Think of some of the tables that bring back memories of special people and events in your life. Some tables have the ability to bring back rich memories that embrace us in warm remembrance of loved ones no longer with us. Just now I can remember sitting at my grandmother's kitchen table as a child, watching her roll out dough. When I am in an antique shop and see one of those metal-legged Formica tables, I instantly remember my grandmother. I remember the cloud of flour dust that engulfed the table, the thud and squeak of the wooden rolling pin as the dough was rolled out, getting to sample a small piece before it became a properly baked pie.

Some tables are more ominous. They can cause us great anxiety and fear. Have you ever been on an operating table? The room it sits in is uncomfortably cold. You have to arrive very early in the morning, and prior to surgery, you can't eat for hours. Someone goes over the risks involved as you try to get comfortable and stay modest in a poor-fitting gown. Someone smiles down at you from behind a mask and says, "Try to relax." These are tables we would rather avoid if they were not absolutely necessary.

Some tables cause awkwardness and disorientation. Think about a student trying to find a table in the lunchroom on their first day of middle school. They have to navigate an elaborate web of social norms and relational constructs. A wrong choice can send the student down a path from which their social status may never recover. At least, that's what's racing through the student's mind at the time.

Different tables conjure up different memories, emotions, and thoughts, depending on the context.

Pause for Reflection

What comes to mind as you consider each one of the following tables?
- Kids' table.
- Breakfast table.
- Defendant's table.
- Thanksgiving table.
- Mortician's table.
- Picnic table.

- Bridal party table.
- Table of the Lord.
- Carpenter's table.
- Card table.

Our experiences and backgrounds have shaped our responses to hearing their names spoken. It is helpful to consider the context of the table that David references in the familiar lines of Psalm 23: "He prepares a table before me."

Fred Wright has said, "In the lands of the East, when a host accepts a man to be his guest, he thereby agrees at whatever the cost to defend his guest from all possible enemies during the time of his entertainment." He goes on to recount the experience of an American missionary who was serving in the East:

> Dr. Cyrus Hamlin was being entertained by a governor. The host took a piece of roast mutton and handed it to the missionary, saying as he did so, "Now do you know what I have done?" In answering his own question, he went on to say: "By that act I have pledged you every drop of my blood, that while you are in my territory no evil shall come to you. For that space of time, we are brothers."[92]

This extreme sense of hospitality is birthed out of the customs of the ancient Near East. Guests were thought of as gifts from the Lord Himself. A high level of appreciation and honor were bestowed on those who shared the host's table. As an Eastern proverb says, "Every stranger is an invited guest … while in the house of its lord."[93] Suffice it to say, it was no small thing to be the guest of an important host; even more so, to be the happy guest of the Lord Himself.

For David to sit at the table prepared by the Lord, he must be an honored guest under the protection of the Lord. Even in the presence of his enemies, he was at peace, secure, and safe. The story of Cyrus and the governor, cited in the passage above, is hauntingly relevant in an apostolic reading of Psalm 23. Jesus offers every drop of His blood in order to secure our protection and our place at the table of the Lord.

In 1 Samuel 9, we see David imitating the Lord's gracious hospitality. After defeating King Saul and ascending to the throne of Israel, David pledges that Mephibosheth, the son of Jonathan and grandson of Saul, will always have a place at the king's table. This was an *extraordinary* declaration. In David's day, it would have been normal, perhaps even expected of him, to have every member of Saul's family banished or executed because of their potential claim to the throne. David broke with the cultural norm and at his table, offered protection to Mephibosheth.

Today's world could benefit greatly from imitating the gracious hospitality of the Lord. Imagine a world in which we became champions of the peace, security, and safety of those we share community with. Never underestimate the tremendous power of hospitality.

In a recent *Christianity Today* article, Sandra McCracken shared a story of friends who, while serving as missionaries, splurged on the purchase of a large table. The table became a focal point, illustrating their priority of hospitality. "Community orbited around the table through conversations, feasting and regular time spent face to face over meals."[94] She ends her article with this beautiful phrase: "Setting out plates and forks can become a liturgy of fellowship ... when we gather, God's Spirit infuses hope into the rhythms of our lives." Something powerful happens when we exercise the gift of hospitality as an extension of the Lord's gracious invitation of inclusion. McCracken's story stands apart as an exceptional experience and not at all common in our increasingly isolated world.

Researchers have discovered that "people who eat socially are more likely to feel better about themselves and have a wider social network capable of providing social and emotional support."[95] Alarmingly, we often understand the benefits of sharing the table with others, but rarely experience it. The same researchers have noted that, "more than two thirds (69 percent) of those questioned had never shared a meal with any of their neighbors, 37 percent had never eaten with a community group, while a fifth of people said it had been more than six months since they had shared a meal with their parents." Knowing that the Lord offers us space at His table should be a call to the church to become a place of gracious invitation.

It is my prayer that we accept the Lord's invitation to come to the table that has been prepared for us and that as the recipients of this gracious hospitality, we would extend the same to those who the Lord has called us to serve. We in The Salvation Army are blessed with countless tables. Let's press them into service as extensions of the Psalm 23 table, prepared and ready for those who would accept the Lord's invitation.

PREPARATION

If you have been responsible for setting a table for guests in your home, or perhaps been a part of a team setting up for a large banquet at your church, you have an appreciation for the work involved in setting a table. The more formal the occasion, the more elaborate the setting can become. As I write this chapter, we're only weeks away from the Thanksgiving holiday, which is traditionally when we put extra time and effort in setting the table for a feast with invited family and friends. I confess that when I am responsible for setting the table at home, I often search the internet for pictures of table settings to refresh my memory as to where each piece rightly belongs. I should be able to remember, but the truth of it is that I do not, so I rely on others to set the example for me. I do admire those who are naturally gifted as hosts. They know the order in which to lay out the cutlery, how to order the plates, and how to tell the difference between a relish spoon and a bullion spoon. They are masters at designing and arranging the perfect centerpiece for any occasion. I have one friend who is an especially gifted host. She was recently called home to be with the Lord, but while on Earth, she made it her goal to ensure that those who entered her home knew that she was expecting them. I am sure that after parting from this life, she was welcomed with open arms and a wonderful table set in preparation for her arrival. The Lord was expecting her, too. One day He will receive you, one of His sheep, with the same hospitality.

There are a few things we should note about the nature of the Lord in the role of the host. Psalm 23:5 opens with four important words: "You prepare a table ..." The key word of emphasis here is "prepare." David could take comfort in knowing that the Lord had prepared for him. God was ready for David. He was not an unwelcome or unwanted guest; he was expected. Our presence does not surprise God. The Lord is ready and prepared for it. We are given some insight into this part of the Lord's character all throughout Scripture. Consider the words of Jesus to His disciples just before His ascension into heaven. "Let not your hearts be troubled. Believe in God; believe also in me. In my Father's house are many rooms. If it were not so, would I have told you that I go to prepare a place for you?" (John 14:1-2). Knowing that the Creator of the universe has prepared for us has the power to quiet troubled hearts. There are plenty of things in this world that can trouble our hearts, but none of these can catch the Lord off guard. He is prepared for anything.

When we consider preparation in the context of the Near East tradition of David's time, which has continued as part of today's Bedouin culture, a beautiful picture of hospitality emerges. A stranger journeys to an encampment through the vast expanse of wilderness; they are noticed from a long way off. While they are still a barely recognized figure on the horizon, the preparation for their arrival begins. When the weary traveler finally reaches the camp, a great banquet has already been prepared and the traveler is treated as an honored guest.

ABUNDANCE

As David describes the hospitality that he encounters as a welcome guest at the Lord's table, he also alludes to abundance. He says that his cup overflows. There is the abundance of a finely set table, but even more so, there is the abundance of the divine. The very presence of the Lord is more than we, as mortals, can take in. His presence fills us past our capacity. As one writer has said, "The Lord's goodness towards His children never ends and their cup will forever overflow, for Jesus emptied Himself by taking upon Himself our flesh, our sufferings and our sins on the cross."[96] It is at the intersection between the human and the divine that we discover just how overwhelming the presence of the Lord is. It stunned Moses, ruined Isaiah, rendered Zechariah speechless, and knocked Paul to the ground. For David, it manifested in a vision of a table and cup far beyond those fit for a king.

When we are invited to join the Lord at His table, we must be prepared to be overwhelmed. Whatever your capacity is, it will be overflowed by the immeasurable presence of the Shepherd-King.

CHAPTER 10
YOU ANOINT MY HEAD WITH OIL

> *"See how good and how pleasant it is for brothers to live together in unity! It is like the precious oil on the head, that ran down on the beard, even Aaron's beard; that came down on the edge of his robes; like the dew of Hermon, that comes down on the hills of Zion: for there Yahweh gives the blessing, even life forever more." –Psalm 133:1-3*

Oil was one of the most critical resources of the ancient world. It was used for food, cooking, lamp oil, medicines, currency, and for important civic and religious ceremonies. In a large majority of the time oil is mentioned in the Old Testament, it is in reference to olive oil. To quantify this, 176 of the 191 times that oil is mentioned in the Old Testament are specifically in reference to olive oil. It should not be surprising that olive oil is referenced so frequently when oils are mentioned in the Bible. "Ancient documents in Syria indicate that around 2000 BCE the value of olive oil was five times that of wine and two and a half times that of seed oils."[97]

In Psalm 45:7, a psalm belonging to the descendants of Korah, the writer references the "oil of gladness." They write, "You love justice and hate evil. Therefore God, your God, has anointed you, pouring out the oil of joy on you more than on anyone else."[98] Charles Spurgeon preached a sermon on this passage, noting the manner of operation upon the believer by this oil of gladness. He lists eight of them:

- We are anointed into a priestly fellowship.
- We are consecrated by the Lord.
- We are qualified to the office which the Lord has called us to.
- The anointing acts as a healing balm which brings about restoration.
- The anointing strengthens us.
- The oil acts as a beautifier.
- It acts as a perfume, enabling others to recognize the Spirit in us.[99]

The first occurrence of olive oil in the Old Testament comes in the middle of a controversial and convoluted story of blessing. Jacob has, with the help of his mother, just received a blessing from his father Isaac by deception (Genesis 27). The blessing had been meant for his brother Esau. It was a stolen blessing taken by the power of crafty deceit. This theft came at the heavy cost of banishment. Following the deception, Jacob was sent away for a two-fold purpose; firstly, for his own safety, and secondly, to take a wife from his maternal uncle's family. It is during this flight to Padan-Aram that while sleeping, Jacob has the vision of a ladder reaching up into the heavens. The Lord spoke to Jacob during this dream, or vision, and blessed him with the same words of blessing that he had received earlier from his father. This is significant, as the initial blessing was garnered by questionable and deceptive measures. That is to say, the first blessing was stolen. This time, the blessing was intended specifically for Jacob and therefore, was devoid of the initial theft's deception. It is in response to this vision and blessing that Jacob sets up a memorial stone and anoints it with olive oil. Genesis 28 captures this moment for us: "Then Jacob awoke from his sleep and said, 'Surely the Lord is in this place, and I did not know it.' And he was afraid and said, 'How awesome is this place! This is none other than the house of God, and this is the gate of heaven.' So early in the morning Jacob took the stone that he had put under his head and set it up for a pillar and poured oil on the top of it."[100] This becomes the first in a long line of anointings, or blessings, commemorated by the pouring on of olive oil.

Did you catch how the rock was used before it became an anointed-memorial stone? As a pillow! An important lesson here is that rocks make less than ideal pillows. Using a rock for a pillow is a recipe for a sleepless night, but perhaps the rock pillow is a helpful metaphor for what had happened in Jacob's life. Firstly, there was the rock pillow of living a lie based on the deception of his father. Sowing seeds of deception and lack of integrity have caused many sleepless nights. Then, there was the rock pillow of the broken relationship between Jacob and Esau, which haunted Jacob for decades, causing heartache and anxious worry for him nearly all his life. There is something very unsettling about the breakdown of relationships that disrupts our sleep and causes our hearts to grow cold. Ruth Graham once said, "When we allow our hearts to grow cold, we unknowingly put ourselves in a precarious spiritual position. For when our hearts glaze over and shut down, when we no longer feel, we run the risk of our love growing cold."[101] The rock pillow of an uncertain future exists as a popular cause of sleepless nights, too. Remember that Jacob left both the comfort and vocation of his home. He was on the road toward something entirely new and different. Perhaps you can relate to journeying toward the unknown. Beginning a new job or appointment, facing retirement, taking on a new project, starting a family, dealing with the loss of a spouse, opening a business. These represent several circumstances that launch us into the unknown. While I write this chapter, the United States is experiencing what has been called the "Great Resignation." The Bureau of Labor Statistics has estimated that on average, a staggering 3.9 million Americans quit their jobs each month in 2021. There are a great number of individuals that are placing their head on rock pillows and experiencing a lot of sleepless nights.

The very stone that had been a source of sleepless nights for Jacob had now become a monument in his life, marking an important moment in his journey. Jacob setting up the stone and anointing it with oil represents God's grace, blessing, and direction in his life. It is sometimes in the most sleepless and challenging moments of our lives that we find grace and direction. We can look back on those moments as memorial markers along the history of our lives that remind us of the Lord's provision.

For David, the image of having his head anointed with oil was more than a beautiful metaphor that tied into Israel's history. It had deep personal significance for him. When Saul's time as king of Israel began to crumble beneath his feet, God sent Samuel to identify Saul's successor. After careful inspection of all of Jesse's sons, David was called out of the fields of his father in order for Samuel to see him. The Lord made it clear that it was David whom He had chosen to become the king of Israel. In response to the Lord's leadership, Samuel anointed David on the spot:

> "Then Samuel took the horn of oil and anointed him in the midst of his brothers. And the Spirit of the LORD

rushed upon David from that day forward. And Samuel rose up and went to Ramah."[102]

This anointing probably made quite an impression on young David. I am sure that as David wrote Psalm 23, and said, "The Lord anoints my head with oil," his mind drifted back to the day Samuel poured out the horn of oil on him. What David did not know as he was being anointed all those years ago, and what he began to understand as he wrote Psalm 23, was that anointing brings with it brokenness, responsibility, healing, and blessing, each in its own time and profound way.

In central Missouri there is an emerging wine industry. There are acres of vineyards that have been carefully planted. According to experts, the long, hot summers and good soil are ideal for growing the grapes used to produce wine. A few years ago, I arranged a meal for my leadership team at a restaurant located in the heart of one of these vineyards. We chose a particularly busy night for our meal and parking was at a premium. I finally found a parking spot in the back of the venue where the meal was to be held. When I opened the door of my car, there was an enormous buzzing; it was deafening. Next to the building was a large dumpster serving as a receptacle for crushed grape skins used in the production of wine. It seemed this dumpster was what was buzzing, but actually, it was the swarm of bees that were attacking the dumpster. The bees were in heaven, busy extracting a bounty from the brokenness. The scene of broken and crushed grape skins was far from the elegance of the front of the restaurant. However, that was the cost of producing the wine. There was a breaking that was necessary in the production of something of immense value, and this concept is true of the production of oil as well.

A breaking was necessary to capture the oil that filled the horn of Samuel. Olive oil is not a naturally occurring substance. The oil is held deep in the meat of the olive. The olives themselves must be broken, crushed, and have pressure applied to them in order to harvest the precious oil that they contain.

In the time of David, and right up until the first century, the common method of harvesting olive oil involved pulverizing the olives themselves, then gathering the broken fragments and collecting them into large porous sacks. The sacks were then stacked as many as ten high into hollow stone columns. Running through the column was a long beam that was hinged at one end. The beam would fulcrum out six to ten feet. On the protruding length of the beam, stones would hang from ropes to add weight to the beam, acting as a lever to apply tremendous weight. The process would squeeze or press the bags tightly to extract the oil from the olive mash. The pressure was great so as not to waste even a drop of the precious oil.

Over his life, particularly after he was anointed as the future king of Israel, "David was often under immense pressure;"[103] pressure from Israel's enemies, pressure from the mad king who sought to destroy him, and even pressure from within his own family. You can hear it in David's often repeated lament to the Lord: "How long will you people ruin my reputation?" (Psalm 4:2); "O Lord, how long will you forget me? Forever?" (Psalm 13:1); "O Lord, how long will this go on? Will you hide yourself forever?" (Psalm 89:46). We can understand this lament.

We have even added *our* voices to it at times. "How long will these struggles and disappointments last? How long will we have these financial difficulties? How long will these health issues persist? How long will the difficulties in this relationship last? How long will I struggle with this addiction? How long will these intense temptations last? How long will it take me to get over this loss? How long until this pandemic is over? We understand something about brokenness. Those of us who have answered the call to ministry can relate to David's call of "How long?" We can sometimes fool ourselves into thinking that our anointing for mission and ministry is a free pass from suffering and brokenness. The exact opposite is often the case.

The anointing of David did not act as a shield from pain and brokenness. His anointing was a commencement into brokenness and heartache. One writer has eloquently captured the emotion of the brokenness that came as a result of David's being anointed. Gene Edwards notes, "Then do you find it strange that this remarkable event led the young man not to the throne but to a decade of hellish agony and suffering? On that day, David was enrolled, not into the lineage of royalty but into the school of brokenness."[104] This anointing of David was an invitation into a life of pain. One cannot dismiss that there was great joy and an overwhelming sense of mission as the leader of Israel. However, as any leader can testify to, leadership is an invitation to suffering. There are painful decisions that only the leader can make. Leading comes at a cost. It can cost friendships and relationships, and even nights of sleep. Remember the rock pillow? The heavy weights of responsibility and duty hang from the beam of leadership and press down hard on the shoulders of the leader.

Take the example of Jesus. There is no better illustration of the heavy weight of leadership and responsibility than that of Jesus. In Mark 14, Jesus is only hours away from being heartbreakingly betrayed, cruelly beaten, wrongfully arrested, and ultimately, brutally crucified. In the dark hours of the night leading up to these events, Jesus walked up the steep hill to a place called Gethsemane to pray. With His three closest followers and friends near Him, He confessed that His soul was "sorrowful, even unto death" (Matthew 14). The name of the olive vineyard where Jesus collapsed in sorrowful prayer is significant. It illustrates the brokenness and pressure of this critical moment in Jesus' life. Gethsemane can be literally translated to mean "oil press."

At the place known as "the press," Jesus had laid on the crushing weight of every sin in the world, past and future. The weight of this pressed down heavy on His soul, a gravity incomprehensible to the human mind. When I consider just the challenges of my own life and its shortcomings, Jesus' actions are overwhelming. When we are pressed by the challenges of this world, "our 'Abba! Father!' experience of God's Spirit, then, thrusts us back to Jesus in Gethsemane sprawled out upon the ground and crying out to God."[105] We can take heart in the fact that Jesus has already modeled the way for us. His willingness to be subjected to the weight of our sin produces for us the ability to be reconciled with the Father. It is in our "Abba! Father!" moments that we find fellowship with our Savior's sufferings. It is often in the excruciating moments of our lives, when we are pressed down upon, that some of the choicest fruit is produced in us. As much as we would like to avoid the pain and stress associated with the pressure, we grow because of it. As the Apostle Paul has said, "For as we share abundantly in Christ's sufferings, so through Christ we share abundantly in comfort too" (2 Corinthians 1:5).

Anointing is never a superfluous action. It is intended to convey responsibility. When Samuel poured the horn of oil over the head of David, the responsibility of leadership was poured over him at the same time. Often it is difficult to know the full extent of the implications of a calling. David didn't know the full extent of what he would have to face after his anointing from Samuel. Officers in The Salvation Army do not know all that they will face over the course of their officership, as they stand on the platform and are commissioned, ordained, and given their first appointment. Leaders cannot envision all that they will face when they are launched into leadership roles. What is true is that the ramifications of the commissioning ceremony, and the mantle of leadership, carry an incredible responsibility. In the past year, a number of my officer colleagues have found that pressure to be too much, resigned, and sought vocations that offer lighter weights of responsibility.

The anointing or calling is only the starting point. It is an important and significant moment, but it signifies the responsibility that will follow. For David, it would be a decade after his anointing before he could commence with the responsibility to which he had been called. It would also be a lifetime before he could fully understand and appreciate its full significance. Reflecting on the calling to ministry, Tom Marshal has written, "Leaders must have confidence. They need confidence in God, in their calling to leadership, and as part of that calling, the ability to find within themselves and in their personal spiritual walk, the resources of courage, faith, or hope that they and their people will need."[106] Calling and ordination are only the starter gun for those called into ministry. Anointing is synonymous with sending; it is a commencement into the mission of God to bring restoration to creation. Anointing is never an end unto itself. David was not anointed only to remain in Jesse's fields attending his sheep. He was off to slay a giant, comfort a king, become a man of war, and lead God's people.

Sending is the Lord's go-to plan at every significant juncture of biblical history. When it is God's intention to intervene in this world, He always sends. As God was raising up a new leader for Israel, He sent a shepherd. When David moves into this part of the psalm, he doesn't entirely abandon the shepherd metaphor. A careful examination of Middle Eastern shepherding and their use of oil among their sheep can be particularly helpful to the reader of Psalm 23. One writer, who has extensively studied the art of ancient shepherding, has shed some light on how the healing properties of oil would have been employed by shepherds for their sheep. Timothy Laniak notes, "One ancient remedy for parasitic tormentors was olive oil. Rubbing it around the nose and eyes of an animal would create a protective coating. The ancient's aspirin, oil, was used as a general salve for most injuries."[107] As was mentioned earlier, the shepherd was both protector and physician for his sheep. The wilderness can be an unrelenting place. Both insects and injuries can prove to be anywhere from frustrating to fatal. The wise shepherd uses his oil to protect his sheep from the opportunistic parasite and to nurse injured sheep back to health.

David's rule as king of Israel was not immune to opportunistic parasites, that is, those who sought to take advantage of their relationship with him. Some of them were those who he loved and trusted the most. One of the most notable was an unlikely parasite— a trusted advisor of David's named Ahithophel. The Bible celebrates his wisdom and immense leadership ability by stating that the "counsel that Ahithophel gave was as if one consulted the word of God…"[108] Initially, he is not a likely suspect.

However, when you understand that Bathsheba was his granddaughter, it sheds more light on the relationship between him and David. When David is expelled from the palace by his son Absalom, it is Ahithophel who recognizes an opportunity to exact revenge on David for tarnishing the honor of his granddaughter. He asks Absalom for 12,000 men to pursue and kill David (2 Samuel 17:1). The once trusted advisor to David now desires to send out a hunting party to bring swift justice to an embarrassed and banished fugitive. However, David has been anointed and protected by the Good Shepherd. God thwarts the plans of Ahithophel. As David protected his sheep by anointing their heads with oil, so God protected David. Some believe it is likely that this story of Ahithophel played out in real time as David wrote Psalm 23.

Perhaps you have some parasites who seek to dismantle that which God has called you to do. Some are easily identified, but others are well disguised, hidden in plain sight. Take heart in knowing that the Lord has anointed your head with oil. He has set you apart and put His protection on you. This does not mean that you will not experience injuries along the way. It is also not a guarantee that you will not experience pain, heartache, and loss in the service of the Lord. Just as a shepherd tends to the wounds of sheep with oil, God's anointing becomes a salve for *our* wounds. God reveals a part of His nature to us through the vision that He gives to John in the Book of Revelation. He invites those who are blind, naked, and shamed to have their eyes anointed with healing salve in order that they might see (Revelations 3:18). It is a beautiful picture of the healing nature of God. It is a picture that is closely aligned with the image of the Lord as shepherd. If you have been wounded or hurt, God offers healing and restoration. Because of our relationship as sheep of the Good Shepherd, He calls us to be restored by His healing anointing.

There is an intimacy between the shepherd and the sheep—those who are receiving and those who are applying the anointing. It is impossible for a shepherd to apply oil to his sheep without getting close. Once while on vacation in Florida, my wife and I were attending a small corps. During the service, the corps officer began to describe an illness that he was struggling with. He moved off the platform and knelt between the two rows of pews and looked at me. We had met briefly before the service, and he knew that we were visiting officers. Without any warning, he announced that I was going to anoint him with oil and pray for his healing. This brought the concept of being ready *in season and out of season* to a whole new level. What can you do in a moment like that? The officer *did* have his own oil which made the anointing a bit easier. I prayed for him and anointed his head with oil. I had prayed for others who were ill before, but only at arm's distance. This was different; it was a close-quarters prayer. It was hands-on ministry. God is a close-quarters shepherd. "Whatever the condition [of the sheep], shepherds can't simply stand at a distance. They need to touch the sheep … to be checked individually for signs of illness, wounds, or weight loss. Such preventative, precautionary, proactive measures only happen with direct physical contact."[109] I thank the Lord that He is a close-quarters Shepherd. He calls us in close to heal every wound and to hold us close.

For David the implication is clear. God intends to bless others through the anointing that is placed on him. Immediately after David was anointed, we read in Scripture that God's Spirit left

Saul and he began to tumble down the hole of madness. Those who were close to Saul started searching for some way to bring the king relief. They had a plan, but it was dependent on finding someone skilled. David, who was blessed by God, was the obvious choice. 1 Samuel 16 records for us how David was perceived: "One of the young men answered, 'Behold, I have seen a son of Jesse the Bethlehemite, who is skillful in playing, a man of valor, a man of war, prudent in speech, and a man of good presence, and the Lord is with him'" (1 Samuel 16:18). God's anointing had helped others see the blessings that had been given to David. He was a skilled musician, unusually bravehearted, a skilled fighter, an eloquent speaker, and he made a good first impression. These blessings were not given simply to make David an impressive young man. These blessings were pressed into service to help Israel through an increasingly precarious moment in history. Not only were the blessings that David received useful in comforting a mad king, but they were also essential for his bravery to face and defeat a giant that had held an entire nation hostage. The lesson we learn is that we are blessed in order to bless others.

We see this principle illustrated early on in Scripture. As Abram is called by the Lord to set out from his hometown to the land the Lord will show to him, he receives a blessing from the Lord. One might call this an anointing. This blessing is not simply a gift to Abram in recognition of his faith. God intends something bigger here. The Lord intends to form a nation on which to place His affection and blessing. The initiation of this desire to create and bless a nation is the blessing of an individual: Abram. "Leave your native country, your relatives, and your father's family, and go to the land that I will show you. I will make you into a great nation. I will bless you and make you famous, and you will be a blessing to others" (Genesis 12:1-2). God blesses Abram in order that he might be a blessing. All the blessings of Israel start with the blessing of Abram (Genesis 12:1-3).

When the Lord anoints your head with oil, it should be understood as God's intention to bless you. God pours His love and affection onto you as one who is dearly loved. But it doesn't stop there; it moves out to those who you have connections with. As Israelites made their way up to the temple to worship, they would recite a number of psalms, known as the Psalms of Ascent, to prepare themselves to be in the presence of God. One of those psalms (Psalm 133) is a beautiful picture of the concept of God's anointing and blessing moving out from an individual and into a community. The psalmist says, "Behold, how good and pleasant it is when brothers dwell in unity! It is like the precious oil on the head, running down on the beard, on the beard of Aaron, running down on the collar of his robes!"[110] The implication is that when the believers come together in unity, the Lord's anointing is contagious. Eugene Peterson described it this way, "Living together means seeing the oil flow over the head, down the face, through the beard, onto the shoulders of the other—and when I see that I know that my brother, my sister, is my priest. When we see the other as God's anointed, our relationships are profoundly affected."[111] When we are anointed and blessed by the Lord, it is also the Lord's intention that we bless others. Our whole mindset toward others is transformed. We begin to see others as those whom God desires to bless. It is a profound mystery why God chooses to allow us to become instruments of those blessings. It begins with a recognition that we are truly blessed. Once we have settled that in our hearts and minds, the whole world takes on new dimension. Those who walk into our doors are sons and daughters of the Lord on whom He desires to pour His oil of blessing. Those we work with are no longer seen as competition but rather as those who God wants to lavish His blessing on. As believers ourselves, we are the first ones called to model this community of those blessed in order to *be* a blessing. Dietrich Bonhoeffer wrote, "The Christian needs another Christian who speaks God's Word to him."[112] We need each other. Your brothers and sisters in Christ need your blessing, and you need theirs. Imagine what your church, your city, or this nation might look like if we could see one another as those worthy of God's love, affection, and blessing. Imagine if we began to demonstrate God's desire to bless others.

Who has God called you to bless today? It is not always the most likely choice. Remember, Samuel went through *all* of Jesse's older and stronger brothers until the Lord told him to look at David.

Pause for Reflection

- If what Bonhoeffer says is correct, "the Christian needs another Christian who speaks God's Word to him," to whom do you need to speak God's Word?

- Who is speaking God's Word to *you*?

CHAPTER 11

GOODNESS AND MERCY SHALL FOLLOW ME

"No matter what barriers you may have erected in his way, The Lord never stops pursuing you." –Ben Cerullo

David begins the final verse of Psalm 23 with the words, "Surely goodness and mercy will follow me all the days of my life." The Hebrew word that David uses for "follow" is *a'har*, or *radaph*, both understood to mean "a pursuit which overtakes." *The Complete Jewish Bible* translates this portion of the verse this way: "Goodness and grace will pursue me every day of my life…" In *The Message* paraphrase of this verse, Eugene Peterson tried to capture the Jewish sense of the phrase by writing, "Your beauty and love chase after me." The Passion translation says it this way: "For your goodness and love pursue me all the days of my life. Then afterward, when my life is through, I'll return to your glorious presence to be forever with you!" All three of these versions of Psalm 23:6 choose to use the most literal understanding of the verb: to pursue or chase. Daniel Emery writes, "God's goodness and mercy are not passively hanging around behind us. They are actively pursuing us. They are chasing us down. Like a lion hunting its prey, so too the goodness and mercy of God are hounding us." Have you ever thought of God as pursuing you, chasing you down, or overtaking you? David understood goodness and mercy (love) as a relentless pursuer in his life.

It is the incredible love of God, our Lord Shepherd, that compels Him to chase after us. The Lord relentlessly searches for us.

Like a lover who at any cost risks it all to be near the one they dearly love, the Lord follows us. The songwriting team of Caleb Culver, Cory Asbury, and Ran Jackson capture this sentiment in their song "Reckless Love":

> "Oh, the overwhelming, never-ending, reckless love of God/ Oh, it chases me down, fights 'til I'm found, leaves the ninety-nine/ And I couldn't earn it, I don't deserve it, still You give yourself away…"[113]

It is incredible to imagine that the Creator of the universe has such an intense love for us that He recklessly pursues us. Still, we have a love-hate relationship with being pursued. Children erupt with jubilant laughter if they can convince their parents to chase them around the house. School children have devoted hours to robust games of tag in the school yard. But it can be heart-stopping and terrifying to be the target of an *unwanted* pursuit. I recently purchased a new bike. It was time; my old bike was purchased used nearly ten years ago and was showing its age. Lots of tender care had been given to the old bike over time, but I discovered that the technology had changed dramatically over the years. My new bike was superior in many ways to my previous bike. Riding the new bike brought back the joy and fear of bike riding in my youth. I can still vividly remember the incredibly aggressive neighborhood dog who would harass me as I rode by the fence that separated him from me. Even more vividly, I can remember when that dog escaped the confines of his yard and pursued me as I was riding my bike. My legs began churning the pedals of my 5-speed lime-green bike as fast as they could. I kept a vigilant eye on the pursuing dog who, despite my efforts, was gaining precious ground on me. I can still hear the sound of the front wheel of the bike being folded into a pretzel-like shape as I crashed into the back of a parked car. In a fraction of a second, I was launched airborne. The car didn't move an inch; it was the early 70s and cars were more like tanks than the cars of today. The crash stunned me and confused the dog. He made his way to where I was laid out on the ground and with a wagging tail licked my face. I had misread the intention of the dog and his pursuit. What I interpreted as murderous intent, the dog saw as a playful game of tag. Sometimes, we misread the Lord's pursuit only to discover that He has good intentions for us.

The Lord pursues people in part because we are very good at running away. Like how I misread the intentions of the dog, we can misread the intentions of the Lord and run from Him. The good news is that He is relentless in His pursuit and intends to overtake us. The Bible has multiple references to individuals who initially ran from God only to eventually be overtaken by His goodness and love.

Jonah, one of the most infamous biblical runners, was overtaken in the middle of the ocean on a wave-beaten ship. Those who were on the same ship "knew that he was fleeing from the presence of the Lord, because he had told them" (Jonah 1:10). The city of Nineveh was overtaken by the goodness and love of the Lord only after the reluctant prophet stopped running (Jonah 4:2).

King Saul was overtaken by the goodness and love of the Lord while running for cover and hiding under a pile of suitcases on the day he was to be anointed as the first king of Israel (1 Samuel 10:21-22).

Elijah, after a stunning victory and miraculous signs, ran and hid himself under a broom tree, where the goodness and love of the Lord caught up with him (1 Kings 19).

It took forty years for the Lord to overtake Moses, who had run to the wilderness of Midian. Moses became the embodiment of the Lord's pursuit of His people, who were living as captives in Egypt at the time (Exodus 2).

Even brave Peter could not get out of the courtyard fast enough when he was recognized as one of Jesus' disciples during Jesus' trial. After His resurrection, the goodness and forgiveness of the Lord overtook Peter. Not only that, but Jesus also invited the restored Peter to the pursuit of others (Matthew 26 and John 21).

As the great and perfect Shepherd, the Lord pursues His sheep; even those who are reluctant to be overtaken. Quantrilla Ard notes, "There is nothing we can do to escape this beautiful benefit of being a sheep under the care of a good Shepherd."[114] The Lord's goodness and mercy pursues us relentlessly and constantly. Ard goes on to say, "You can't outrun His goodness to you. You can't sprint fast enough that mercy, His loving-kindness, won't overtake you. So slow down and receive it."[115] This is a hard lesson for some to receive. In part because we have a warped sense of who the Lord is and what His intentions are. However, if we are willing to "receive it," what a blessing it is for His sheep who decide to stop running and become overtaken. One of the incredible opportunities that we have within The Salvation Army and other Christian ministries is bearing witness to those special moments in which the Lord's goodness and mercy catches up to those who have been on the run for a very long time. We can encourage the wearied runners to slow down and receive the loving embrace of the Lord. Perhaps it is you who is still running. Take heart; your Lord Shepherd is pursuing you. He isn't far behind you; He is ready to overtake you with a refreshing gift of goodness and love.

The Lord's goodness and mercy also follows us in another way. Because of our relationship to the Lord Shepherd, we leave evidence of His goodness and mercy in our wake. A Salvation Army missionary once noted that when a missioner is sent out into the world, the missioner is forever marked by the experience. Their life is forever transformed by the time, the people they interact with, and the Lord's provision for them while they are serving. In addition, the mission field itself is marked because of the presence of the missioner. It too will never be the same. This is a sobering thought for those who are embarking on this type of work.

Here's a humorous anecdote to illustrate the point. I recently worked with an officer who moved to the United States from the Philippines, a place where my wife and I had served a few times on short-term missions. Our lives were never the same because of the experience. When we were there, we did not meet this officer; it was only after she arrived in the U.S. and to the same division that I was appointed to that we were able to meet. But she informed me that I was, in her words, quite famous in the Philippines. Before I could fully embrace the pride of being famous, she told me why. One of the more reliable forms of transportation in the Philippines is called a tricycle. It's a small motorcycle driven by one person and fitted with an outrigger that holds a passenger pod for others to sit in. Since the passenger area was far too small for me to fit into, I decided to stand on the bumper of the vehicle and ride in a standing position. In doing so, the outrigger became somewhat of a teeter-totter so the driver and his motorcycle were lifted off the ground. The combined weight of myself and the passenger pod were too much for the driver and his motorcycle. Of all the things I had hoped to leave as a memory on the mission trips, this was not the one I intended. This is a good reminder to us all that we will leave something in our wake as we serve, but first and foremost, we should endeavor to leave the love and mercy of the Lord.

It should bring us a great deal of comfort to know that the Lord is with us, our constant companion along this journey through life. We know from the Word that the Lord intends good for us and extends His mercy toward us. It is a blessing to know that His pursuit of us is relentless. Even in times when we are unaware of His presence, He is close. Many have discovered, when reflecting on their faith journey, that they have benefitted from a long history of the Lord's constant and abiding presence in their lives. Sometimes it appears as flashes and moments of individual moments. But a retrospective examination of the life of a believer reveals a long and enduring chain of the Lord's presence and pursuit. We can share this witness with others who feel far from God and presently do not feel His presence. Our witness can serve as an assurance that the Lord is interested in them and seeks to engage them with His love and mercy.

I have found that those who seek to keep God at a distance have a common perception of His character. They share a notion that the Lord is a God of judgement. In some ways, this is profoundly true. God is the divine judge of all things. However, this perception can cloud the fact that the Lord is also the God of *mercy*. It creates an unfortunate false dichotomy: that the Lord is either completely judgmental or completely merciful. The truth is that the Lord is perfectly both. In addition, the Book of James tells us that "there will be no mercy for those who have not shown mercy to others. But if you have been merciful, God will be merciful when he judges you."[116] This seeming paradox contains a profound truth: at the interception where judgement and mercy meet, mercy prevails. As you read this passage in its larger context, it admonishes Christians who cling to one part of the law while ignoring other aspects of it. James makes it clear that any violation of the law, despite how many other aspects are followed, still exposes believers to judgement. God is merciful; due to the sacrifice of Jesus Christ, we are recipients of God's mercy and grace.

What James understands is that even though we deserve judgment, the Lord's goodness and mercy pursues us. Or, as David has mentioned, they follow us all our days. What a welcome idea. There is not a single day that passes in which the goodness and mercy of the Lord doesn't pursue us and relentlessly run after us. I would guess that this truth has the potential to impact some of the people you have been called to serve and minister to. Perhaps it is something that encourages your soul today.

Pause for Reflection

- Have you ever thought of the Lord as pursuing or chasing after you?

- Give some thought to the lyric, "… chases me down, fights till I'm found." What does it mean that the Lord fights until you are found?

- When have you been a recipient of God's mercy?

CHAPTER 12
I SHALL DWELL IN THE HOUSE OF THE LORD FOREVER

I read a brief article recently about an ancient cemetery in the Italian city of Pisa. A group of well-intentioned Christians arranged for a shipment of soil from the Holy Land to be brought to the cemetery so that people could be buried in the "terra sancta," or holy ground. It was thought that being buried in this special soil added additional power to salvation; that this terra sancta would supercharge their journey to heaven as their eternal dwelling place. There is seemingly no limit to the clever ways in which mankind seeks any advantage in its quest for immortality. Interestingly, David's final words in Psalm 23 have an eschatological focus. In them, David looks toward eternity with the exuberant expectation of spending it with the Lord. David's benediction to Psalm 23 is an affirmation, "I will dwell in the house of the Lord forever."

The Hebrew verb that David uses here for the word "dwell" is *swb*. Its most literal translation means "to make linear motion back to a point previously departed." Throughout the Old Testament, much of the time the verb is used to denote a sense of returning or bringing back. In Genesis 8, it is used to describe Noah reaching out his arms from the window of the ark to gather a storm-beaten dove. He "brought her" back into the ark because she found no shelter on the flooded earth. In Genesis 28, Jacob has his famous ladder dream in which the Word of the Lord comes to him and says that He will "bring [Jacob] back" to this land which had been promised to Abraham. Both Ezra and

Jeremiah speak of a time coming when the Lord will "bring back" both the land and its people. Isaiah proclaims, "And now the LORD speaks—the one who formed me in my mother's womb to be his servant, who commissioned me to bring Israel back to him..." (Isaiah 49:5). "Bringing back" is the overwhelmingly consistent way in which this verb is used in the Old Testament. Translating *swb* to mean "dwell" is extremely rare. Of the 1,048 times the word is used, it's only in Psalm 23 that it is translated to mean "dwell."

Why would David, a masterful writer, choose this word? There are four variations of *swb* that I think may be helpful in understanding what David is saying in Psalm 23. Each provides the reader with a unique perspective of the word.

Return

The first variation involves return. The thought of going back to the place from which one has departed is a part of the Easter story. After Jesus rose from the dead and appeared to the women in the garden, He tells them not to cling to Him, for He has not yet ascended or been brought back to the Father (John 20). Jesus is soon going to ascend to the place He has come from and belongs, to be in the presence of the Lord. David's use of this unique verb helps us to understand that the place where he desires to be is in the presence of the Lord. Keep in mind that when David wrote Psalm 23, the Temple, which is thought of as the house of the Lord, was yet to be constructed. The plans for it were in the mind and heart of David, but at that point, the house of the Lord represented an ethereal and spiritual state rather than a physical location.

The place where David sought to dwell is where his soul recognized its real home. The Christians of Pisa were trying to get a head start on their journey home by using soil from the Holy Land. While this did not make a bit of difference for the saints from Pisa, we can appreciate their sentiment. The great promise of Easter is that we have a home not in this world but prepared for us by Jesus, who invites us to return to this place to be with Him. Miraculously, we are invited to dwell there even now while we are still residing in this world.

LINEAR MOTION

The second variation addresses the idea of a linear motion. It is a wonderful visual image. No detours, no distractions. Go directly home. Do not pass "go." Do not collect $200. My parents used to tell me these things when they wanted me to come home right away. I knew that I was expected to come straight away without delay. David understands where it is that he desires to be. As one commentary writer has put it, "Of all the places where the psalmist might choose to be, he longs to stay in God's presence all his days." David understood the awesome and everlasting invitation to be in the Lord's presence without witnessing Easter for himself. How much more should you and I desire to dwell in the presence of the Lord knowing that Jesus has made a way for us. I love the way the song writer captures this desire to be in the presence of the Lord,

"Your presence goes before us,

Your glory has no end,

God, You never leave me."[117]

While the world we live in seeks to distract us from what is really important, let us keep our focus on the goal of our hearts: the eternal presence of our God.

Previously Departed

If we consider when this psalm was written, while David was on the run in the wilderness, we can detect a certain homesickness. His father's fields or the comforts of his palace would have been welcome places for him to return. However, these places from which David departed did not compare to his desire to be in the Lord's presence. His real home, his real place, was in the Lord's presence. You can hear his desperation to be in the Lord's presence in other psalms as well. "Do not banish me from your presence, and don't take your Holy Spirit from me. Restore to me the joy of your salvation, and make me willing to obey you. Then I will teach your ways to rebels, and they will return to you" (Psalm 51:11-13). Perhaps you have already realized that the words "return" and "restore" used in this passage are also words David uses in Psalm 23 in place of the word "dwell."

I pray that the Lord would kindle in your heart a desire to be in His presence; for the Lord to reach out with His gentle hands and bring you back to His comforting presence. This is your real home; the place your soul has been created to dwell in. May you, like David, make the beautiful affirmation that you will dwell in the house of the Lord forever.

Pivot

This understanding of the word we see as "dwell" is used also in the Book of Joshua. After a deadly and embarrassing battle loss for Israel at the hands of a small kingdom called Ai, the Lord provided Joshua with a strategy to take the city. The Israelite forces were divided into two groups. One that would mimic the failed frontal attack previously employed, and one that would hide and ambush Ai when its warriors went out to attack Joshua and the army of Israel. Joshua 8:21 records what happened. "When Joshua and all the other Israelites saw that the ambush had succeeded and that smoke was rising from the town, they turned and attacked the men of Ai."[118] What had not worked in the past had to be rethought out, and Israel had to pivot by using a different approach. The concept of pivoting has been invoked many times in the past couple of years as the world has had to react to a global pandemic. Some have suggested that the word has even been overused. But we can appreciate that this idea of pivoting invokes a sense of going a different direction. It is easy to ride the waves of complacency, carried by the momentum of this world. However, we are called to be different. We are built to be in the Lord's presence. It may be time for you to pivot and change your direction so that you may be brought into the welcome embrace of the Lord's presence.

These variations help us to appreciate what David is saying in Psalm 23. He is banished, embarrassed, and on the run. He desires to pivot, turn around, and in linear motion, return to where he belongs. This place he desires to be, he pictures as the house of the Lord. It is here where he envisions dwelling forever. It is a place of still waters, green pastures, and the ever-present company of his Lord Shepherd.

Pause for Reflection

- Of the ways in which the word "dwell" has been described above, which is the most meaningful to you now?

Final Thoughts

I trust that as we have studied this psalm together, you have gained a new appreciation for an old and familiar chapter of Scripture. I am also hopeful that your understanding of the Lord as our Shepherd has been broadened. Perhaps the next time you hear Psalm 23 read, you will recall some of the lessons we have discovered. It is likely that the next time you hear it, you may be at a funeral, as this is where it's reheard often. But I am enlisting you in an effort to liberate it from those confines; help others to gain an appreciation for the imagery of this psalm.

I leave you with a paraphrase of Psalm 23 that draws on the expanded understanding we have gained in this journey together. May it help us to move past the over-familiarity with Psalm 23 and afford us an opportunity to hear God speak in a new and fresh way:

The Lord is my Shepherd-King,

Because you are my Shepherd, I have everything I need.

You have caused me to lie down in pleasant green pastures.

You lead me to the places where the floodwaters are stilled.

You make me whole, a soul restored to its original glory.

You guide me in the ways of holiness.

When I find myself in the very deep shadows, surrounded by death, I reach out Lord, and you are there, right with me.

When I see your rod and staff, they assure me of your presence and bring me comfort.

You invite me, as an honored guest, to a table you have prepared for me. No enemy can harm me when I am there with you.

You pour your anointing oil over my head, preparing me for a life of following you.

Your affections, they chase after me. I cannot escape your love.

I cease my wandering and turn around, run back to you, to the place I belong, and never let go. I want to be near you, to move into your house and stay there forever, a permanent resident in the Lord's house.

ENDNOTES

1 *The Bible Knowledge Commentary: An Exposition of the Scriptures* by Dallas Seminary Faculty. (p. 81).
2 Soltau, Henry W. *The Tabernacle: The Priesthood and the Offerings*. Grand Rapids, MI: Kregel Publications, 1972.
3 Montonini, M. (2012, 2013, 2014). *Shepherd*. In J. D. Barry, L. Wentz, D. Mangum, C. Sinclair-Wolcott, R. Klippenstein, D. Bomar, … D. R. Brown (Eds.), The Lexham Bible Dictionary. Bellingham, WA: Lexham Press.
4 Frye, Northrop. *The Great Code: The Bible and Literature*. New York: Harcourt Brace Jovanovich, 1982.
5 Keil, C.F.; Delitzsch, Franz (2014-06-22). *Commentary on Psalms* (Kindle Locations 5085-5086). Kindle Edition.
6 Brengle, "When the Holy Ghost Is Come."
7 Tyndale House Publishers, *Holy Bible: New Living Translation* (Carol Stream, IL: Tyndale House Publishers, 2015), Mt 2:6.
8 v. 15.
9 Hebrews 13:20.
10 Revelation 17:20.
11 Needham, Phil, *Community in Mission: A Salvationist Ecclesiology* (summarizing: William A. Clebsch and Charles R. Jaekle).
12 Broyles, Craig C. *Psalms (Understanding the Bible Commentary Series)* (p. 124). Baker Publishing Group.
13 Mt 7:9–11.
14 Ge 22:2.
15 Heb 11:17–19.
16 Genesis 22:14.
17 Tyndale House Publishers, *Holy Bible: New Living Translation* (Carol Stream, IL: Tyndale House Publishers, 2015), Ps 121:4.
18 Ps 77:20.
19 Ro 13:1.
20 Ex 12:39.
21 Laniak, Timothy. *While Shepherds Watch Their Flocks: Forty Daily Reflections on Biblical Leadership*.
22 Heb 10:11-12.
23 Philippians 4:19.
24 Peterson, Eugene H. *A Long Obedience in the Same Direction: Discipleship in an Instant Society*. IVP Books.
25 Cocklin, T. *Dayenu* (p. 1).
26 *Salvation Army Ceremonies*. The Salvation Army.

27 John 21:17.
28 Dongell, J. (1997). *John: A Bible commentary in the Wesleyan Tradition* (pp. 248–249). Wesleyan Publishing House.
29 Blum, E. A. (1985). John. In J. F. Walvoord & R. B. Zuck (Eds.), *The Bible Knowledge Commentary: An Exposition of the Scriptures* (Vol. 2, p. 345). Wheaton, IL: Victor Books.
30 Harold Begbie (2013). *The Life of General William Booth*. MacMillan. Retrieved from https://app.wordsearchbible.com.
31 1 Peter 5:8.
32 Psalm 68:5.
33 1 Samuel 17:32 (ESV).
34 Luke 22:39-42.
35 Earl Guthrie, "History of Veterinary Medicine," Iowa State University Digital Repository, https://lib.dr.iastate.edu/iowastate_veterinarian/vol2/iss1/1.
36 Ezekiel 34:4.
37 Ezekiel 34:16.
38 Hughes, R. B., & Laney, J. C. (2001). *Tyndale Concise Bible Commentary* (p. 452). Wheaton, IL: Tyndale House Publishers.
39 Hughes, R. B., & Laney, J. C. (2001). *Tyndale Concise Bible Commentary* (p. 452). Wheaton, IL: Tyndale House Publishers.
40 (Eze 34:1–4).
41 Greeven, H. (1964–).. G. Kittel, G. W. Bromiley, & G. Friedrich (Eds.), *Theological Dictionary of the New Testament* (electronic ed., Vol. 2, p. 892). Grand Rapids, MI: Eerdmans.
42 Acts 1:8.
43 Swanson, J. (1997). *Dictionary of Biblical Languages with Semantic Domains: Hebrew (Old Testament)* (electronic ed.). Oak Harbor: Logos Research Systems, Inc.
44 Daniel 5:27.
45 Walvoord and Zuck. *The Bible Knowledge Commentary*, (p. 134).
46 1 Samuel 13:13.
47 Keil, C. F., & Delitzsch, F. (1996). *Commentary on the Old Testament* (Vol. 5, p. 207). Peabody, MA: Hendrickson.
48 Williams, Donald (2004-07-30). *Psalms 1-72: Psalms 1-72: 13 (The Preacher's Commentary)* (Kindle Location 3877). Thomas Nelson. Kindle Edition.
49 Matthew 7:3.
50 New York Post: https://nypost.com/2018/12/21/new-years-resolutions-last-exactly-this-long/.

51 http://www.nrcs.usda.gov/wps/portal/nrcs/detail/wi/technical/cp/cta/?cid=nrcs143_014209.
52 David, Christopher Poshin. *The Shepherd and Me.*
53 (Steppesoffaith 2019).
54 https://www.forbes.com/sites/forbescoachescouncil/2018/12/07/why-work-harder-not-smarter-is-silently-destroying-your-business-results/#17ea6311422b.
55 IBID.
56 https://rickwhitter.com/2017/11/18/dangers-for-pastors/.
57 Crosby, Fanny, "Rescuing the Perishing", *Salvation Army Songbook 2015.*
58 Booth, William., 509, "O Boundless Salvation! Deep Ocean Of Love", *Salvation Army Songbook 2015.*
59 Guder, Daniel L., Lois Barrett. *Missional Church: A Vision for the Sending of the Church in North America.*
60 Keller, W. Phillip. *A Shepherd Looks at Psalm 23* (p. 48). Zondervan.
61 IBID.
62 Laniak, Timothy. *While Shepherds Watch Their Flocks: Forty Daily Reflections on Biblical Leadership.* ShepherdLeader Publications.
63 Swanson, J. (1997). *Dictionary of Biblical Languages with Semantic Domains: Hebrew (Old Testament)* (Electronic ed.). Oak Harbor: Logos Research Systems, Inc.
64 Wesley, John (1950). *The Journal of John Wesley* (p. 292). WORDsearch. Retrieved from https://app.wordsearchbible.com.]
65 Miller, Basil (2014). W7-5199 *Holiness* (Catherine Booth).
66 Samuel Logan Brengle (2014). SA-2939 *Heart Talks on Holiness.*
67 *Come Thou Fount*, Robert Robinson.
68 Tyndale House Publishers, *Holy Bible: New Living Translation* (Carol Stream, IL: Tyndale House Publishers, 2015), Jn 1:1.
69 Krol, Peter. *Knowable Word: Helping Ordinary People Learn to Study the Bible.* Cruciform Press, May 2014.
70 Lennox, S. J. (1999). *Psalms: a Bible commentary in the Wesleyan tradition* (p. 80). Indianapolis, IN: Wesleyan Publishing House.
71 Barnes, Albert. *Notes on the Old Testament: Psalms, vol. 1* (London: Blackie & Son, 1870–1872), 211.
72 IBID.
73 Carr, Kurt. *I Almost Let Go.*
74 Tyndale House Publishers, *Holy Bible: New Living Translation* (Carol Stream, IL: Tyndale House Publishers, 2015), Ac 7:55-60.
75 Thank you to Colonel Susan Harfoot who is the granddaughter of Captain Lillie May Hodge for recounting this extraordinary story.

76 Harfoot, Susan.
77 Samuel Logan Brengle (2013). *Heart Talks on Holiness*. Salvation Army.
78 Keller, W. Phillip. *A Shepherd Looks at Psalm 23* (p. 77). Zondervan.
79 Barnes, Albert. *Notes on the Bible*. (1834).
80 *American Standard Version*. 1995. Oak Harbor, WA.
81 Psalm 122:6-9.
82 Hebrews 13:5.
83 Mathans, Walter John. *God is With Us*. SA Song Book 923 (1985).
84 Bailey, Laura. "Eternity Changes Everything," February 2022. https://proverbs31.org/read/devotions/full-post/2022/02/04/eternity-changes-everything.
85 Lille, alain de , sermo de sphaera.
86 Kierkegaard in Hemati, Christi Lyn, PhD.
87 Romans 8:18.
88 Proverbs 3:11-12.
89 Hebrews 12:11 (ESV).
90 Eze 20:37.
91 Ritenbaugh John W. *Forerunner Commentary*.
92 Wright, Fred H. *Manners and Customs of Bible Lands*. 1953.
93 Turnbull, Clay. *Oriental Customs, Traditions & Social Life*. 1988.
94 McCracken, Sandra. "The Dinner Table: Don't Pack Away the Dinnerware During COVID-19." *Christianity Today*, 21 Dec. 2021, pp. 30–30.
95 The University of Oxford: https://www.ox.ac.uk/news/2017-03-16-social-eating-connects-communities.
96 David, Christopher David. "The Shepherd and Me." *Devotional Reading Plan | YouVersion Bible*, You Version Bible, https://my.bible.com/reading-plans/23207-the-shepherd-and-me.
97 Vossen, Paul, 2007/08/01, *Olive Oil: History, Production, and Characteristics of the World's Classic Oils*.
98 Tyndale House Publishers, *Holy Bible: New Living Translation* (Carol Stream, IL: Tyndale House Publishers, 2015), Ps 45:7.
99 https://www.blueletterbible.org/Comm/spurgeon_charles/sermons/1273.cfm.
100 Genesis 28:16-18.
101 Graham, Ruth. *In Every Pew Sets a Broken Heart*.
102 1 Samuel 16:13.
103 *Bible in One Year 2020 With Nicky Gumbel*.
104 Edwards, Gene. *A Tale of Three Kings* (pp. 6-8). Tyndale House Publishers, Inc.
105 Lodahl, Michael. *The Story of God: A Narrative Theology* (*updated*).

The House Studio.
106 Marshall, Tom. *Understanding Leadership* (p. 160). Baker Publishing Group.
107 Laniak, Timothy. *While Shepherds Watch Their Flocks: Forty Daily Reflections on Biblical Leadership*. Shepherd Leader Publications.
108 2 Samuel 16:23.
109 Laniak, Timothy. *While Shepherds Watch Their Flocks: Forty Daily Reflections on Biblical Leadership*. ShepherdLeader Publications.
110 Psalm 133:1-2.
111 Peterson, Eugene H. *A Long Obedience in the Same Direction: Discipleship in an Instant Society*. IVP Books.
112 IBID.
113 "Reckless Love of God." Bethel Music.
114 https://proverbs31.org/study/online-bible-studies/Psalm-23/blog/2019/10/09/goodness-mercy-and-the-chase.
115 Ibid.
116 James 2:13.
117 Wade Joye / Mack Donald Iii Brock / Christopher Joel Brown / London Gatch / Steven Furtick / Jane Wood Williams. In Your Presence. Elevation Worship, 2013.
118 Joshua 8:21.

BIBLIOGRAPHY

Ard, Quantrilla. "Goodness, Mercy and the Chase." *Proverbs 31 Ministries*, https://proverbs31.org/study/online-bible-studies/Psalm-23/blog/2019/10/09/goodness-mercy-and-the-chase.

Bailey, Laura. "Eternity Changes Everything," February 2022. https://proverbs31.org/read/devotions/full-post/2022/02/04/eternity-changes-everything

Barrett, Lois, and Darrell L. Guder. *Missional Church: A Vision for the Sending of the Church in North America*. William B. Eerdmans, 2009.

Begbie Harold. *Life of General William Booth, the Founder of The Salvation Army*. Hardpress Ltd, 2013.

Booth, Catherine. *Holiness*. The Salvation Army, 1881.

Brengle, Samuel Logan. *Heart Talks on Holiness*. Salvationist Publishing & Supplies, 1949.

Brengle, Samuel Logan. *When the Holy Ghost Is Come*. Project Gutenberg.

Broyles, Craig C. *Psalms*. Baker Books, 2012.

Clebsch, William A, and Charles R Jaekle. *Mission: A Salvationist Ecclesiology*.

Cocklin, T. *Dayenu: A Christian's View of Passover with the Haggadah*. Worlds of Wonder Publishing, 2014.

David, Christopher David. "The Shepherd and Me." *Devotional Reading Plan | YouVersion Bible*, You Version Bible, https://my.bible.com/reading-plans/23207-the-shepherd-and-me.

"DSpace Angular Universal." *DSpace Angular :: Home*, https://lib.dr.iastate.edu/iowastate_veterinarian/vol2/iss1/1.

Frye, Northrop, and Alvin A. Lee. *The Great Code: The Bible and Literature*. Penguin, 2014.

Graham, Ruth, and Stacy Mattingly. *In Every Pew Sits a Broken Heart: Hope for the Hurting*. Zondervan, 2008.

Gumbel, Nicky. "Bible in One Year 2020 with Nicky Gumbel." *Devotional Reading Plan | YouVersion Bible*, https://my.bible.com/reading-plans/17704-bible-in-one-year-2020-with-nicky-gumbel#!.

Hemati, Christi Lyn. "The Concept of Eternity in Kierkegaard's Philosophical Anthropology."
Texas Digital Library, 2009. https://baylor-ir.tdl.org/bitstream/handle/2104/5342/Christi_Hemati_phd.pdf;sequence=1.

"History—Iowa State University." Vetmed.iastate.edu, vetmed.iastate.edu/about/history.

Holy Bible: English Standard Version. Crossway Bibles, 2001.

Holy Bible: New American Standard. Broadman & Holman, 1977.

Holy Bible: New International Version. Zondervan, 2008.

Hughes, Robert B., et al. *Tyndale Concise Bible Commentary.* Tyndale House Publishers, 2001.

Keil, Carl Friedrich, and Franz Delitzsch. *Commentary on The Old Testament.* Hendrickson Publishers, 2011.

Keller, W. Phillip. *A Shepherd Looks at Psalm 23.* Zondervan, 2018.

Kittel, Gerhard, et al. *Theological Dictionary of the New Testament.* Eerdmans, 2006.

Krol, Peter. *Knowable Word: Helping Ordinary People Learn to Study the Bible.* Cruciform Press, May 2014.

Laniak, Timothy S., and David Ormesher. *While Shepherds Watch Their Flocks: Rediscovering Biblical Leadership.* Shepherd Leader Publications, 2007.

Lennox, Stephen J. *Psalms: A Bible Commentary in the Wesleyan Tradition.* Wesleyan Pub. House, 1999.

Lodahl, Michael. *Story of God: A Narrative Theology.* Beacon Hill Press, 2010.

Marshall, Tom. *Understanding Leadership: Fresh Perspectives on the Essentials of New Testament Leadership.* Baker Books, 2003.

Montonini, M, et al. *Shepherds.* Lexham Press, 2014.

"Natural Resources Conservation Service." *Grazing Lands | NRCS Wisconsin,* http://www.nrcs.usda.gov/wps/portal/nrcs/detail/wi/technical/cp/cta/?cid=nrcs143_014209.

News.com.au. "New Year's Resolutions Last Exactly This Long." *New York Post,* New York Post, 22

Dec. 2018, https://nypost.com/2018/12/21/new-years-resolutions-last-exactly-this-long/.

O'Donnell, Suz. "Council Post: Why 'Work Harder, Not Smarter' Is Silently Destroying Your Business Results." *Forbes*, Forbes Magazine, 7 Dec. 2018, https://www.forbes.com/sites/forbescoachescouncil/2018/12/07/why-work-harder-not-smarter-is-silently-destroying-your-business-results/#17ea6311422b.

Peterson, Eugene H. *A Long Obedience in the Same Direction: Discipleship in an Instant Society*. IVP Books, an Imprint of InterVarsity Press, 2021.

Ritenbaugh John W. *Forerunner Commentary*. https://www.bibletools.org/index.cfm/fuseaction/Topical.show/RTD/cgg/ID/6452/Rod-Passing-under-the.htm

Rivett, Reggie. "The Paths of Righteousness Have a Shadow to Them." *Christian Thought Sandbox*, 24 Oct. 2018, christianthoughtsandbox.wordpress.com/2018/10/24/the-paths-of-righteousness-have-a-shadow-to-them/. Accessed 27 June 2023.

Salvation Army Ceremonies. Manitoba Education and Advanced Learning, Alternate Formats Library, 2014.

The Salvation Army. *The Song Book of the Salvation Army*. Salvationist Publishing and Supplies, Ltd., 2015.

Soltau, Henry W. *Tabernacle, the Priesthood, and the Offerings*. Nabu Press, 2010.